Testing with F#

Deliver high-quality, bug-free applications by testing them with efficient and expressive functional programming

Mikael Lundin

[PACKT] open source*

PUBLISHING

community experience distilled

BIRMINGHAM - MUMBAI

Testing with F#

First published: February 2015

Production reference: 1170215

Published by Packt Publishing Ltd.
Livery Place
35 Livery Street
Birmingham B3 2PB, UK.

ISBN 978-1-78439-123-2

www.packtpub.com

Credits

Author
Mikael Lundin

Reviewers
Neil Danson

Max Malook

Karlkim Suwanmongkol

Commissioning Editor
Amarabha Banerjee

Acquisition Editor
Reshma Raman

Content Development Editor
Shweta Pant

Technical Editor
Tanmayee Patil

Copy Editors
Gladson Monteiro

Merilyn Pereira

Nithya P

Project Coordinator
Sageer Parkar

Proofreaders
Simran Bhogal

Lauren E. Harkins

Indexer
Tejal Soni

Graphics
Sheetal Aute

Abhinash Sahu

Production Coordinator
Shantanu N. Zagade

Cover Work
Shantanu N. Zagade

About the Author

Mikael Lundin is a software developer living in Malmö, Sweden. He started programming in Pascal 20 years ago and has been enjoying the craft both professionally and as a hobby through languages and frameworks such as PHP, C#, F#, Ruby, and Node. He has been a practitioner and mentor of test-driven development and agile methodologies for the last 8 years, helping teams succeed in delivering high-quality software.

Mikael has been working with F# for 4 years, providing solutions to clients, publicly speaking about functional programming, and holding seminars for colleagues to spread the word. He strongly believes that functional programming is the future of delivering high-quality software.

Mikael is employed as a technical consultant by Valtech in Sweden, where he takes on the roles of a software developer, solution architect, and agile mentor. He has delivered quality software to high-profile international clients and helped organizations adopt Scrum as their software development practice.

I would like to thank my employer, Valtech, for always letting me experiment with new technologies and giving me the encouragement to learn and share my knowledge. I also would like to thank my wife, Jenny, for understanding my need to undertake a project that infringed on our time and time with our family. Finally, I would like to thank my colleagues for always being supportive of the challenging tasks I set out to do.

About the Reviewers

Neil Danson is an active professional developer and passionate F# advocate since 2010. He has over 10 years of experience in using the .NET framework, working on varied projects that range from military software and huge-scale international news websites to high-performance trading platforms. When Neil is not working, he can usually be found writing games, compilers, raytracers, and anything else that pops into his head. He can be found occasionally blogging at `https://neildanson.wordpress.com`.

I would like to thank my wife, Carla, for putting up with my obsession with code for so long, and my children Joseph and Matthew, who have yet to learn how to tolerate it. I'd also like to thank the F# community for its vibrancy and its inspiration to learn, promote, and most importantly, have fun with F#.

Max Malook is a software developer with a passion for code quality. He has many years of experience in different programming languages. He recently fell in love with functional programming, especially F#. In his spare time, Max maintains an open source project, FeatureSwitcher, a .NET library for simple feature toggle integration. He also supports other projects such as Humanizer, F# language, FAKE, and Paket.

Max offers consulting and training on software architecture, code quality and review, functional programming, and other topics; feel free to get in touch with him at `http://malook.de`.

I want to thank my wife for being patient with me while I reviewed this book.

Karlkim Suwanmongkol is a correctness engineer at Tachyus, a company that creates technology to optimize energy production for the oil and gas industry. Here, he focuses on software quality and testing using F#. Some time ago, Karlkim developed software for multiple industries, including hospital, defense, university, and gaming. He also contributes to several F# open source projects on GitHub and blogs about new things he learns at `http://karlk.im/`. You can find him on Twitter at `@kimsk`.

I would like to thank my wife, Chanitanon, for her patience with my late night F# coding and reading.

www.PacktPub.com

Support files, eBooks, discount offers, and more

For support files and downloads related to your book, please visit www.PacktPub.com.

Did you know that Packt offers eBook versions of every book published, with PDF and ePub files available? You can upgrade to the eBook version at www.PacktPub.com, and as a print book customer, you are entitled to a discount on the eBook copy. Get in touch with us at service@packtpub.com for more details.

At www.PacktPub.com, you can also read a collection of free technical articles, sign up for a range of free newsletters and receive exclusive discounts and offers on Packt books and eBooks.

https://www2.packtpub.com/books/subscription/packtlib

Do you need instant solutions to your IT questions? PacktLib is Packt's online digital book library. Here, you can search, access, and read Packt's entire library of books.

Why subscribe?

- Fully searchable across every book published by Packt
- Copy and paste, print, and bookmark content
- On demand and accessible via a web browser

Free access for Packt account holders

If you have an account with Packt at www.PacktPub.com, you can use this to access PacktLib today and view 9 entirely free books. Simply use your login credentials for immediate access.

Table of Contents

Preface

When I started out with unit testing in 2007, I made every imaginable mistake there is. I didn't understand how to isolate my tests from database calls. I didn't understand how to structure my tests. I had no idea what constituted a good test and what should be tested. It was a train wreck, and even if my test suite was pretty much useless, I still found I had gained a lot of knowledge of the system while trying to test it. So, for the next project, I gave it another go.

Once again, in my second project, I failed at writing unit tests. They where brittle, unmaintainable, and quite useless as they would only run under conditions that where reproducible solely on my developer machine. But even if the test suite was crap, the project itself was a success and the code produced was considered to be of very high-quality.

So, I went at it again and again and again, every time coming up with a slightly better end result, until I got to a point where the test suite was a major deliverable of the project, and an enabler for maintenance. However, it took me a long time to get there.

I had been teaching and preaching test-driven development for years, until I began to notice that people around me were doing it, too. I no longer had to justify TDD to people around me, and testing would now be a natural part of any project, and not just something I did on the side. This was splendid, indeed! Mission accomplished!

In 2009, I found out about the F# language from Microsoft Research, and it got my attention. I decided to learn it, and started to hack away during my evenings and weekends to get to the bottom of functional programming. After a while, I felt sure enough to start bringing it into clients' projects. I began with only small snippets at the start, but after a while, the snippets got bigger and bigger, and before anyone knew what was going on, we were implementing services in F#.

For me, test-driven development has been an enabler for quality. It is what enhances the quality in a given project by setting up requirements on the code. The code needs to expose its inner parts in a manner that can be tested in isolation. This leads to good object-oriented design and separation of concerns.

However, at the same time, I had a few worries that the test suite made too large impact on the system design. Why isn't it that we design systems that are testable by default, and why do we need tests to enforce this design thinking?

Functional programming has truly been an eye-opener for me. There is something funny about object-oriented programming I didn't realize before I invested in F# fully. Why is it that I can't create a class in the system without setting up a dependency injection framework? Why do we have all these classes that are cohesive enough that they only do one thing, but that one thing is so abstract that the name of the class is more confusing than informative? Why does every class in the system have an interface identical to the class implementation?

The answer to these questions is that test-driven development has forced these frameworks and patterns onto object-oriented design in order to work together in harmony, but in reality, you end up with a lot of ceremonial code that does very little.

Functional programming is the answer to this question; anyone care to object?

If we stop thinking about systems as interconnected objects and instead see them as functions passing data around, we make our design so much easier. We can skip the dependency injection framework because we don't need to manage an object dependency graph. We do not need interfaces because we can describe functions by their signature. Instead, we can solely focus on the input and what the desired output will be, and from this, we will derive our tests.

While my colleagues struggle with their cloud in the castle abstractions, I produce code that is short, concise, and completely covered. This is the best way to evangelize something better. We do not need to sell functional programming. It sells itself.

Yet, here I have written a book about producing quality code with functional programming and testing. This is a starting point for anyone who is familiar with object-oriented programming and wants to learn about the alternatives that may bring about a more qualitative life as a professional programmer.

I wanted to write this book in order to spread the word and show my peers what huge value they're missing out on by trying to produce value with C# and object orientation alone. My intention is to express the lost love I have found for programming after being stuck in large enterprise code bases where every change would have a ripple of side effects. I want to put this book in the hand of every developer I meet who is asking himself, "How could I do better?"

Your managers will love you for writing less code and getting done at a much faster rate of speed. Your clients will love you for producing code with less bugs. And you will love going to work to deliver code with higher value and less ceremonial waste.

Understanding functional programming and test-driven development are the key points in advancing your career and securing your knowledge base for the inevitable future.

What this book covers

Chapter 1, The Practice of Test Automation, gives an overview of the current field of test automation and an introduction to set the terminology. This chapter will give you a good sense of why test automation is needed.

Chapter 2, Writing Testable Code with Functional Programming, dives into functional concepts in order to write code that promotes testability. This chapter provides you with the introduction to functional constructs that will be used while writing unit tests.

Chapter 3, Setting Up Your Test Environment, acts as a tutorial on setting up your test environment in order for you to start testing, and is focused on tools such as NUnit, xUnit, and the built-in MSTest framework. It also provides a short guide for build scripts and continuous integration with F#.

Chapter 4, Unit Testing, lets you deep dive into unit testing with F# and using functional programming to drive unit tests and testability. It provides examples on how to test in isolation and stubbing, as well as dealing with dependencies and mock away databases.

Chapter 5, Integration Testing, explains how to write good integration tests in F# and what to think about when writing integration tests. We deal with the differences in integration testing with databases to those in external web services.

Chapter 6, Functional Testing, uses tools such as TickSpec in which you can write executable specifications in order to test on a higher abstraction level, which is closer to what the end user will experience.

Chapter 7, The Controversy of Test Automation, brings the reader up to date on what is being said about test automation in the community.

Chapter 8, Testing in an Agile Context, explains how to bring testing into a team and apply it in an agile process. This chapter provides arguments to convince your manager about the benefits test-driven development.

Chapter 9, Test Smells, informs you that just like code smells are an indication of an underlying problem in your design, there are also test smells that indicate there is an underlying problem with your tests.

Chapter 10, The Ten Commandments of Test Automation, covers 10 dos and don'ts of test automation, which comes from 8 years of test-driven development knowledge.

Chapter 11, Property-based Testing, will show you how to get started with FsCheck and it's integration with unit testing frameworks. It will also teach how you can test a game example using model-based testing, which is an extended concept of property-based testing.

This a bonus chapter and can be downloaded from the following link:

```
https://www.packtpub.com/sites/default/files/downloads/_2320S_
Chapter_11.pdf
```

What you need for this book

In order to make full use of this book, you should have a development machine where you can run the latest version of Windows with an installation of Visual Studio Community 2013.

The Visual Studio Community 2013 edition is a fully featured IDE that contains everything you need in order to run the examples in this book and get started with F# development. You can download it from Microsoft at `http://www.visualstudio.com/en-us/news/vs2013-community-vs.aspx`.

There is an even better test runner provided by JetBrains Resharper that will increase productivity when running test-driven development, but it is not necessary for you to learn about in this book. This book will provide only one example of testing with Resharper, and the rest of the examples are done by the built-in tools of Visual Studio Community 2013 at `https://www.jetbrains.com/resharper/`.

Who this book is for

If you are a developer with .NET experience, you will learn through this book how to increase the quality of your deliveries by developing in F# with test automation. Based on what you'll learn, you will benefit from your previous F# experience and also if you've done test automation before in other languages or technologies.

Conventions

In this book, you will find a number of styles of text that distinguish between different kinds of information. Here are some examples of these styles, and an explanation of their meaning.

Code words in text, database table names, folder names, filenames, file extensions, pathnames, dummy URLs, user input, and Twitter handles are shown as follows: "We can include other contexts through the use of the `include` directive."

A block of code is set as follows:

```
// assert
let dbCustomer = CustomerRepository.get customerID
dbCustomer |> should equal newCustomer
```

When we wish to draw your attention to a particular part of a code block, the relevant lines or items are set in bold:

```
let div x y =
  // precondition
  assert(y > 0)
  assert(x > y)
```

Any command-line input or output is written as follows:

```
> parse "MMXIV";;
```

New terms and **important words** are shown in bold. Words that you see on the screen, in menus or dialog boxes, for example, appear in the text like this: "In order to get the path to the library you want to reference, right click on **References** in the **Solution Explorer**."

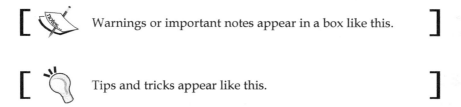

Warnings or important notes appear in a box like this.

Tips and tricks appear like this.

Reader feedback

Feedback from our readers is always welcome. Let us know what you think about this book—what you liked or may have disliked. Reader feedback is important for us to develop titles that you really get the most out of.

To send us general feedback, simply send an e-mail to feedback@packtpub.com, and mention the book title via the subject of your message.

If there is a topic that you have expertise in and you are interested in either writing or contributing to a book, see our author guide at www.packtpub.com/authors.

Customer support

Now that you are the proud owner of a Packt book, we have a number of things to help you to get the most from your purchase.

Downloading the example code

You can download the example code files from your account at `http://www.packtpub.com` for all the Packt Publishing books you have purchased. If you purchased this book elsewhere, you can visit `http://www.packtpub.com/support` and register to have the files e-mailed directly to you.

Errata

Although we have taken every care to ensure the accuracy of our content, mistakes do happen. If you find a mistake in one of our books—maybe a mistake in the text or the code—we would be grateful if you would report this to us. By doing so, you can save other readers from frustration and help us improve subsequent versions of this book. If you find any errata, please report them by visiting `http://www.packtpub.com/submit-errata`, selecting your book, clicking on the **Errata Submission Form** link, and entering the details of your errata. Once your errata are verified, your submission will be accepted and the errata will be uploaded on our website, or added to any list of existing errata, under the Errata section of that title.

To view the previously submitted errata, go to `https://www.packtpub.com/books/content/support` and enter the name of the book in the search field. The required information will appear under the **Errata** section.

Piracy

Piracy of copyrighted material on the Internet is an ongoing problem across all media. At Packt, we take the protection of our copyright and licenses very seriously. If you come across any illegal copies of our works, in any form, on the Internet, please provide us with the location address or website name immediately so that we can pursue a remedy.

Please contact us at `copyright@packtpub.com` with a link to the suspected pirated material.

We appreciate your help in protecting our authors, and our ability to bring you valuable content.

Questions

You can contact us at `questions@packtpub.com` if you are having a problem with any aspect of this book, and we will do our best to address it.

1
The Practice of Test Automation

Test automation is a practice that will make you think differently about coding. A typical non-tester approaches a problem by squabbling about some code in the editor and changing it until it works. Like working with clay, you start from a lump and carefully craft it into a bowl, and once satisfied, let it dry. Once it has dried, there is no way you can change it.

When you start doing test automation, you will quickly identify the key issues with how you've been writing code before:

- You start writing code on a blank sheet without any clear intent on the result
- You don't know when it's time to stop writing code
- You don't know whether your code will keep on working when you add more code

Test automation comes to grips with these issues and provides a process for writing code in a more structured and organized fashion. You start out with a clear intent, implement the code until your tests are green, and refactor it until you're happy with the end result.

Functional programming will open your mind to the flaws in the code you've written previously. You will find that the number of programming errors are reduced when your code becomes stateless. Complexity is reduced by removing the deep object dependency graph from your application. The intent gets clearer when all it consists of is functions and data, where functions operate on data.

Together, test automation and functional programming is a harmonious match that brings together good coding practice with good code, making you, the programmer, fall into the pit of success. By reading this book, you will understand how to combine the two and become a better programmer.

In this chapter, we will cover the following topics:

- What is testing
- The purpose of testing
- Testing with intent
- Writing regression tests

Testing as a practice

Before diving into why we need test automation, we should consider what it really is. The practice is still quite new and there is some confusion surrounding it, leading to developers testing the wrong thing and managers not knowing what to expect.

Black or white box testing

Testing practices are often split into black or white box tests. The difference is distinguished by how much we know about the system we're testing. If all we know about the system is what we can see from the outside and all we can do with it is build outward interfaces, then the method of testing is considered a black box test.

On the other hand, if our testing knows about the inward functions of the system and is able to trigger events or set values within it, then this testing is referred to as white box testing.

These are two slightly different viewpoints to consider when testing. When performing test automation, we need to examine both black and white box testing, where white box testing is closer to the implementation and black box testing is often leaned toward based on a user requirement's abstraction level.

Manual testing

Manual testing is a practice used to investigate a product and determine its quality. This is done by a person called a tester and is performed by executing the program or using a tool to examine it. The testing will validate that the product meets its requirements and determine if the system is usable, but most importantly, it will validate that the product solves the problem it was created for.

The following image shows how testing fits into the normal flow of software development:

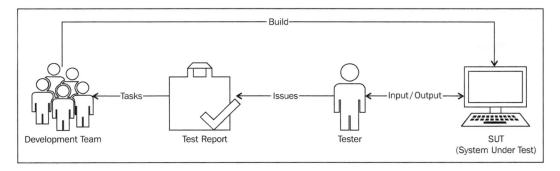

The result of manual testing is a set of issues that gets reported to the development team. Some of these issues are labeled as bugs, defects, or just changes. The tester will rate them based on priority (blocker, critical, high, medium, or low) and incorporate them into the development process.

The term manual testing is usually just called testing, but to avoid confusion, I will refer to testing done by a tester as manual testing and testing that is executed by a computer as test automation.

Test automation

Test automation is a practice used to create checks that will verify the correctness of a product. These checks are written in code or created in a tool, which will then be responsible for carrying out the test. The nature of these checks is that they are based on the requirements and are reproducible through the automation.

The following image shows how test automation doesn't require a tester or need for reports and issue tracking:

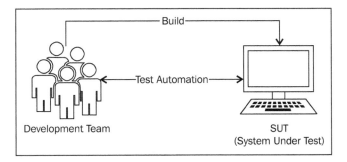

Most commonly, test automation is performed by the development team and is an integrated part of the software development process. It doesn't replace the tester but puts an extra layer of quality assurance between the team and tester, leading to fewer issues reported by the tester.

The best kind of testing is that which requires little effort. The code is reviewed by the computer when compiling the program, verifying that it's possible to turn the code into machine instructions. For a statically typed language, this can be seen as the first line of testing, like a spell check.

Once the code is compiled, the programmer understands that the code will be executed. It will not necessarily do what it's supposed to do, but it's guaranteed to execute, which is not always the case if interpreted at runtime.

The following table shows the layers of testing and what they verify:

Test activity	Input	Verifies
Compiling	Source code	Syntax correctness
Style check	Source code	Code style
Static analysis	Source code / compiled assembly	Code correctness
Unit testing	Compiled assembly	Code correctness
Integration testing	Compiled assembly	Code behavior
System testing	Release version	Product behavior

Style check

A style check on the code will ensure it is properly formatted and enforces conventions such as the name standard, indenting, comments, and so on. This is very valuable in a team setting to increase readability of the code and maximize code sharing, as all developers use the same coding style. The result is higher quality and less friction, leading to fewer bugs and faster development.

For F#, there is a style-checking tool called **FSharpLint**, which is available through the **NuGet** package manager and can be used to check your code against style conventions.

Static analysis

Static code analysis can be used to avoid unnecessary mistakes, including unintended circle references or badly implemented patterns, such as poor implementation **IDisposable**. It helps in avoiding problems that inexperienced developers would have with garbage collection and threading.

There are no good static analysis tools for F# as of this writing. In C#, one could use Visual Studio Code Analysis, previously known as FxCop, for static analysis.

Unit testing

Unit tests are written at the same time as the code, before or after. They verify that the code produces the intended result. This is a form of white box testing that seeks to reduce the number of unintended defects that come out of development. If the unit testing is thorough, the code will do what the programmer intended.

Here's an example unit test:

```
open NUnit.Framework
open FsUnit

[<Test>]
let ``should return 3 from adding 1 and 2`` () =
    Calculator.add 1 2 |> should equal 3
```

Integration testing

An integration test is a test written by the programmer to verify his or her code's integration with other systems or parts of the system, such as databases and web services. The purpose of this testing is to find problems and side effects that only appear in the integration with those other systems. If integration testing is thorough, it will help with the stability of the system.

Here's an example integration test:

```
open NUnit.Framework
open FsUnit

[<Test>]
let ``should store new user to data storage`` =
    // setup
    let newCustomer = { name = "Mikael Lundin"; address =
"Drottninggatan 82 Stockholm" }

    // test, storing new customer to database
    let customerID = CustomerRepository.save newCustomer

    // assert
```

```
let dbCustomer = CustomerRepository.get customerID
dbCustomer |> should equal newCustomer
```

System testing

System testing is a form of black box testing that is performed in order to validate that the system requirements, both functional and nonfunctional, are fulfilled. System testing is a very broad term and is more often pushed to manual testing than it is automated. Executable specifications is one area where system testing automation excels.

Building trust

What you see as a developer when you look at legacy code is distrust. You can't believe that this code is performing its duty properly. It seems easier to rewrite the whole thing than to make changes to the existing code base.

The most common type of bug comes from side effects the developer didn't anticipate. The risks for these are high when making changes in a code base that the developer doesn't know. Testers have a habit of focusing their testing on the feature that has been changed, without taking into account that no change is done in isolation and each change has the potential to affect any other feature. Most systems today have a big ball of spaghetti behind the screen where everything is connected to everything else.

Once, I was consulting for a client that needed an urgent change in a Windows service. The client was adding online payment to one of their services and wanted to make sure customers were actually paying and not just skipping out on the payment step.

This was verified by a Windows service, querying the payment partner about whether the order had been paid. I was going to add some logic to send out an invoice if the online payment hadn't gone through.

The following is the invoice code:

```
// get all orders
OrderDatabase.getAllUnpaid()
|> Seq.map(fun order ->

    // for each order
    let mutable returnOrder = order
    let mutable orderStatus = OrderService.NotSet

    try
```

```
    // while status not found
    while orderStatus = NotSet do
        // try get order status
        orderStatus <- OrderService.getOrderStatus order.Number

        // set result depending on order status
        returnOrder <-
            match orderStatus with
            // paid or overpaid get correct status
            | Paid | OverPaid -> { order with IsPaid = true }
            // unpaid
            | Unpaid | PartlyPaid -> { order with IsPaid = false;
SendInvoice = true }
            // unknown status, try again later
            | _ -> returnOrder
        with
            | _ -> printf "Unknown error"

    returnOrder)

// update database with payment status
|> Seq.iter (OrderDatabase.update)
```

It was implemented and deployed to a test environment in which the logic was verified by a tester and then deployed to production, where it caused €50,000 in lost revenue.

With my failure, I was assuming the `OrderService.getOrderStatus` parameter really worked, when in reality, it failed four out of five times. The way the service was built, it would just pick up those failed transactions again until it succeeded.

My addition to the code didn't take the side effect into account and started to mark most failed payments with the status of `Paid` even though they were not.

The code worked fine while debugging, so I assumed it was working. The code also worked fine while testing, so the tester also assumed it was working. Yet, It was still not enough to stop a crucial bug-hit production.

Downloading the example code

You can download the example code files from your account at http://www.packtpub.com for all the Packt Publishing books you have purchased. If you purchased this book elsewhere, you can visit http://www.packtpub.com/support and register to have the files e-mailed directly to you.

Bad code is that which is poorly written and does not follow best practices by swallowing exceptions and letting the program continue to execute in a faulty state. This makes the code harder to change, and the risk becomes higher as a change could introduce new bugs.

Tests written for a program will guarantee that the code has better structure and is easier to change. This is because tests themselves require well-structured code in order to be written. Unit tests drive code to become better designed with higher quality and easier to read and understand.

Integration tests will verify that code written to integrate with external systems is well-written with all the quirks the external system needs, and regression tests will verify that the intended functionality of a system be kept even after a change has been introduced.

Building trust with programmers is all about showing robustness, and this is done by tests. They lengthen the lifetime of a system, as those systems are open to change. They also shine through to the end user, as those systems will not crash or hang when the unexpected occurs.

The purpose of testing

When starting to learn about test-driven development, many developers struggle with the question: "Why are we doing this?" This is also reflected in the tests they write. They write tests to verify the framework they're using, or for simple trivial code. They also write brittle tests or tests that are testing too much. They have not reflected on why they're testing and often only do it because they've been told to, the worst kind of motivation.

The value of testing is shown in the following image:

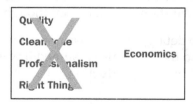

The original illustration comes from a talk by Martin Fowler on refactoring. The title is *Why refactor?* and the same applies to testing. The value of testing comes not from quality, clean code, professionalism, or that it is the right thing. The value is economics. You write tests in order to save money. Bad programming will lead to bugs in your software, which can have the following consequences:

- **Projects running over time**: This is because the team spends time on fixing bugs instead of writing new features. Bugs become a bottleneck for productivity.

- **Corruption of data**: The cost of retrieving lost data or a bad reputation for losing customer data will have substantial economic consequences.

- **System looking unpolished**: Your software will behave irrationally and the users will stop trusting your product. They will take their business elsewhere, to a competitor that doesn't let bad quality shine through.

We need to avoid bugs in order to avoid unnecessary and hard-to-predict costs. By adding testing to our process, we create predictability and reduce the risk to software development projects.

ObamaCare, officially named The Patient Protection and Affordable Care Act, is a law signed on March 23, 2010, in the United States. It was aimed at reforming the American healthcare system by providing more Americans with access to affordable health insurance.

The US government issued a website where people could apply and enroll for private health insurance through ObamaCare. However, the launch of the website was a dead fish in the water.

Not only was the site unable to handle the substantial load of visitors while going live, but it was also having to solve performance problems for several months. The site sent personal information over unencrypted communication, and the e-mail verification system was easily bypassed without any access to a given e-mail account.

An estimation of 20 million Americans experienced the broken ObamaCare site, seriously hurting the reputation of software developers worldwide. By writing tests for our code, we will achieve higher quality, cleaner code, and maintain a higher level of professionalism, but what it eventually boils down to is that the code we write will have greater value. Tested code will:

- **Have fewer bugs**: Bugs are expensive to fix. The code will be cheaper in the long run.

- **Be better specified**: This leads to fewer changes over time. The code will be cheaper in the long run.
- **Be better designed**: Bad code can't be tested. The tested code will be easier to read and less expensive to change.

All of these points of interest lead to predictability, a precious thing in software development.

When not to test

As a part of software development mentoring teams, I tell developers to test everything because they always seem to find some excuse for not writing tests.

Always write tests for your code, except if the following applies; if it does, then it makes no sense to test it:

- The code will never go into production
- The code is not valuable enough to spend tests on
- The code is not mission-critical

The most common excuse developers have for not writing tests is that they claim it is too hard. This holds true until they've learned how to, and they will not learn unless they try.

Testing with intent

There are several angles to go about writing tests for code, and it is important to understand them before you start avoiding some of the bad practices. Tests written without a clear intent by the programmer are often characterized as being too long or asserting too much.

Asserting written code

The most important aspect of unit tests is to assert the code has the intended result when executed. It is important that the author of the tests is the same as that of the code, or some of the intent might be lost in the process.

The following is a code snippet:

```
// System Under Test
let div x y = x / y

// Test
div 10 2 |> should equal 5
```

This might state the obvious, but a developer could easily mix up the order of incoming arguments:

```
// System Under Test
let div y x = x / y

// Test
div 10 2 |> should equal 5
```

Running the test would expose the following error:

```
NUnit.Framework.AssertionException:
   But was:   0
Expected: 5
```

Tests give the developer a chance to state what is not obvious about the code but was still intended:

```
// System Under Test
let div x y = x / y

// Test
div 5 2 |> should equal 2
(fun () -> div 5 0 |> ignore) |> should throw
typeof<System.DivideByZeroException>
```

The test verifies that the remainder of the integer division is truncated, and that the code should throw an exception if you try to divide 5 by 0. These are behaviors that are implicit in the code but should be explicit in the tests.

Writing these assertions is often a faster way to verify that the code does what was intended than starting a debugger, entering the correct parameters, or opening up a web browser.

Contracts versus tests

There is a technique called **Design by Contract (DbC)** that was invented by Bertrand Meyer while designing the Eiffel programming language. The basic idea of DbC is that you create contracts on software components stating what the component expects from the caller, what it guarantees, and what it maintains.

This means that the software will verify the acceptable input values, protect them against side effects, and add preconditions and postconditions to the code at runtime.

The idea of software contracts is very attractive, a few attempts at implementing it for the .NET framework has had limited success. The heritage of DbC is defensive programming, which simply means the following:

*   Checking input arguments for valid values
*   Asserting the output values of functions

The idea behind this is that it is better to crash than to continue to run with a faulty state. If the input of the function is not acceptable, it is allowed to crash. The same is true if the function is not able to produce a result, at which time it will crash rather than return a faulty or temporary result:

```
let div x y =
  // precondition
  assert(y > 0)
  assert(x > y)

  let result = x / y

  // postcondition
  assert(result > 0)
  result
```

Assertions such as these cannot be seen as a replacement for testing. The differences are pretty clear. The contracts are validated at runtime when debugging the code, but deactivated when compiling the code for release. Tests are written outside the main code base and executed on demand.

With good assertions, you'll find more problems when doing manual testing, as the risk of running tests with faulty data is much smaller. You will also get code that is better at communicating its intent when all the functions have a clear definition of the preconditions and postconditions.

Designing code to be written

Testing your code is also an exercise in making it modular to enable it to be called from outside its original context. In doing so, you force the application to maintain an API in order for you to properly test it. It should be seen as a strength of the methodology that makes the code more concise and easier to read. It also enforces good patterns such as the single responsibility principle and dependency injection.

There is a reason for making use of test-driven development using the mantra red, green, refactor. The refactor part of testing is essential to create a successful test suite and application. You use a test to drive the design of your code, making it testable and achieving testability:

```
let rec crawl result url =
    // is duplicate if url exists in result
    let isDuplicate = result |> List.exists ((=) url)

    if isDuplicate then
        result
    else
        // create url
        let uri = new System.Uri(url)

        // create web client
        let client = new WebClient()

        // download html
        let html = client.DownloadString(url)

        // get all URL's
        let expression = new Regex(@"href=""(.*?)""")
        let captures = expression.Matches(html)
                        |> Seq.cast<Match>
                        |> Seq.map (fun m -> m.Groups.[1].Value)
                        |> Seq.toList

        // join result with crawling all captured urls
        List.collect (fun c -> crawl (result @ (captures |> List.
    filter ((=) c))) c) captures
```

This program will get the contents of a URL, find all the links on the page, and crawl those links in order to find more URLs. This will happen until there are no more URLs to visit.

The code is hard to test because it does many things. If we extract functions, the code will be easier to test, have higher cohesion, and also be better in terms of the single responsibility principle.

The following code is an example of extracted functions:

```
// item exist in list -> true
let isDuplicate result url = List.exists ((=) url) result

// return html for url
let getHtml url = (new WebClient()).DownloadString(new System.
Uri(url))

// extract a-tag hrefs from html
let getUrls html = Regex.Matches(html, @"href=""(.*?)""")
                   |> Seq.cast<Match>
                   |> Seq.map (fun m -> m.Groups.[1].Value)
                   |> Seq.toList

// return list except item
let except item list = List.filter ((=) item) list

// merge crawl of urls with result
let merge crawl result urls = List.collect (fun url -> crawl (result @
(urls |> except url)) url) urls

// crawl url unless already crawled it
let rec crawl result url =
    if isDuplicate result url then
        result
    else
        (getHtml url) |> getUrls |> merge crawl result
```

The functionality is the same, but the code is much easier to test. Each individual part of the solution is now open for testing without causing side effects to the other parts.

Writing tests for regression

When developers try to convince managers that testing is something that is necessary to their project, regression is often a card that is drawn. Managers may claim the tests can be run in a build server to make sure functionality is continuously verified. While this is true, it is more of a side effect, unless tests are written for this specific reason.

A good regression test states something about the functionality that is always true. It should not be so much dependent on the implementation but on the specification of the functionality.

I was once working with a client on a system that was fairly complex. It was an order process that was divided into several steps to minimize the complexity for the end user, but still, there were hundreds of business rules implemented in the backend.

I was working alone one evening in the office when a business analyst came rushing in, claiming that I needed to take the website down. After some querying, he told me that the discount logic for students was wrong.

With the business analyst standing over my shoulder, I went into my test suite and found the following regression test:

```
PriceCalc_Should_Discount_Students_With_Child_Under_16_y
o()
```

The test was turning into green as I ran it, and I asked him for his test data. It turned out he was using his own personal information as test data and had a daughter that had recently turned 16.

One peculiar observation about bugs is that they have a tendency to come back, unless carefully observed. This is why it's always best to write a regression on finding a bug to make sure it doesn't reappear. Personally, I write these tests to verify the claim of the bug and then use the test to show me when the bug is fixed.

Executable specifications

Written tests inform from an outside perspective how the system is behaving. This is a very powerful concept that, if enriched, will lead to tests as specifications. Looking at the tests will tell you how the system works.

Having a large test suite could easily replace the requirements and specifications of the system, as the test suite verifies the stated functionality every time tests are run. The documented specifications and requirements become outdated after the first change.

I was once consulting for a client that was going to sell gym memberships online. The implementation itself was not that hard: gather customer information and store it in a **Customer Relationship Management (CRM)** system. The credit card payment was hosted by an external payment provider and integrated with some basic HTTP redirects.

However, the client was insistent on having very complex price logic to a degree where it was impossible for one person to understand why a membership had been assigned a target price.

In order to implement this, I started from the requirements and wrote them all as tests. I felt confident that my test suite covered the whole problem and would implement the system in such a way that my test would turn green.

Turning over the solution to the client for **User Acceptance Testing** (UAT), I got back 10 scenarios where the client claimed the membership had the wrong price.

Still confident in my method of implementation, I chose to implement all failing scenarios as tests. It proved that the code was not wrong, but the logic was so complex that the client couldn't verify it in UAT.

After some iteration with this, the client finally gave up acceptance testing and had us release it to production. As a consultant, I should have advised my client to simplify their price logic.

What tests are trying to achieve as specifications is to have executable specifications written in a natural language that can verify the following:

- The code is implemented as specified
- The code keeps fulfilling the specification (regression)

While specifications are being written in natural language, it is possible for programmers and business analysts to have a common workspace on how the system is supposed to work.

The following example shows the specifications written in a natural language:

```
Feature: Authentication

Scenario: Entering correct login information makes user authenticated
  Given a fresh browser session at http://mikaellundin.name/login
  When entering 'mikaellundin' as username
  And entering 'hello fsharp' as password
  Then browser should redirect to http://mikaellundin.name/profile
```

The specification is written in a **Domain Specific Language** (DSL) called Gherkin. Each line has code connected to it that will execute when the specification itself is executed to verify that the requirement is fulfilled.

Summary

Let's say you're at the airport by the self-service check-in trying to print your boarding card. The machine does not accept your booking number at first, but after a few retries, you're able to check in. After confirming, the machine hangs before printing your boarding card and you're not sure whether you've checked in or not. You move on to the next machine to try again.

In our society today, we put so much of our faith in machines. They handle everything for us, from flying airplanes to shopping online and paying the bills. It is when it doesn't work that we stop in our tracks and reflect on the fact that while the machine might be perfect, the programmer is not.

The reason behind testing is to create stability, predictability, and quality in our software. Writing tests reduces the number of bugs produced and the number of bugs found by our testers.

We write tests to make software cheaper. We do this because bugs are expensive. We do this because change is expensive. And we do this because we would rather go slowly and methodically in the right direction, than very fast down the wrong lane.

In this chapter, we touched upon what test automation is and why it's necessary. The next chapter will look at functional programming and how it makes testing a breeze.

2
Writing Testable Code with Functional Programming

There are three main aspects of writing code in a functional style in F# versus imperative style in a language such as C#:

- No side effects leads to fewer bugs
- Smaller isolated units are easier to test
- Expressiveness makes code right the first time

This chapter will address the following bits about functional programming:

- Purity
- Expressiveness
- Immutability
- Patterns to help you write testable code

By reading this chapter, you will learn how to write high quality code that will become easy to test. This chapter sets the groundwork for how tests will be written in the following chapters.

Purely functional

What is a computer program?

The following image shows the basic working of a computer program:

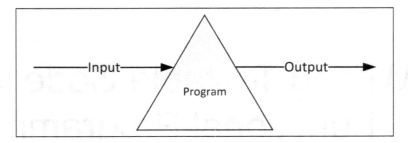

An input computed by a program returns an output. This is a very simple concept but it becomes highly relevant for functional programming.

A former colleague told me that's all there is to it: data and code that operates on data. If you want to take it further, the code itself is also data, so a computer program is really just data operating on data.

What about web programming?

The following image shows the basic working of a web server:

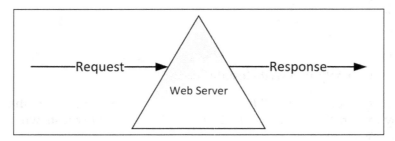

It's really the same thing. You have a web request that the server operates on and returns a web response.

How does this apply to functional programming?

The following image shows the basic working of functional programming:

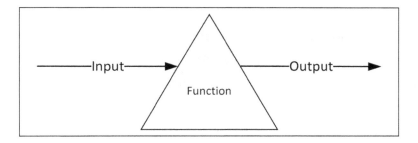

A pure function is very much a computer program. It has an input and output, but the computation of the output adhere to certain conditions:

- The same output is always guaranteed for the same input
- The evaluation of the output cannot have side effects

This means the function cannot depend on any state outside the function scope. It also means that the function cannot affect any state outside the function scope. Actually, the computed output cannot depend on anything else other than the input arguments. All arguments sent to the function should be immutable so they don't accidentally depend on or modify a state outside the function scope.

This means any of the following cannot happen in a pure function:

- Database calls, insert, update, select, and delete
- Web service calls
- Reading or writing to the hard drive

Logging, console output, updating **User Interface (UI)**, and user input are examples of a pure function

```
// reverse a string
let rec reverse = function
| "" -> ""
| s  -> s.[s.Length - 1].ToString() + (reverse (s.Substring(0,
s.Length - 1)))
```

This code reverses a string using the fact that a string is an array of characters, picking each character from the end of the string and joining it by reversing the rest of the string.

Examples of other pure functions are:

- The `sin(x)` function
- The `fibonacci(n)` function
- The `List.map()` function
- The `md5(s)` function

The pure function concept maps perfectly to mathematics. It could be visualized as a simple graph:

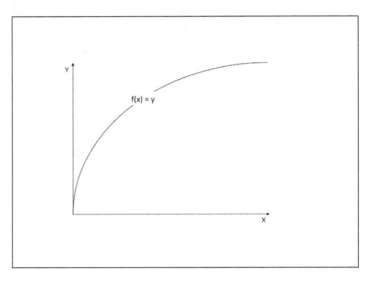

If we consider functions in our programs to work much like the math graph example, we will get a better understanding of how to create simple and straightforward programs.

This doesn't sound like any business software that you know. Do pure programs only happen in fantasy? What is the point of having pure functions?

The advantages of pure functions come in terms of quality because a function that is pure becomes easier to test. There is a universe of possible input, the function arguments for which will generate consistent output with no side effects.

Some tests for the pure reverse function mentioned earlier are as follows:

```
[<Test>]
let ``should reverse 'abcde' as 'edcba'`` () =
```

```
      reverse "abcde" |> should equal "edcba"

[<Test>]
let ``should reverse empty string as empty string`` () =
      reverse "" |> should equal ""
```

Most of the bugs in software development come from the mutating state and side effects because these are very hard to predict. We can avoid these bugs by writing large parts of our programs as pure functions and isolate the need for a mutating state. This would give our code a clearer focus with isolated functions and higher cohesion.

This is one way of increasing testability with functional programming.

Immutability

The default behavior of F# when using the `let` keyword is an immutable value. The difference between this and a variable is that the value is not possible to change. With this, there are the following benefits:

- It encourages a more declarative coding style
- It discourages side effects
- It enables parallel computation

The following is an example implementation of the String.Join function using a mutable state:

```
// F# implementation of String.Join
let join (separator : string) list =
    // create a mutable state
    let mutable result = new System.Text.StringBuilder()
    let mutable hasValues = false

    // iterate over the incoming list
    for s in list do
        hasValues <- true
        result
            .Append(s.ToString())
            .Append(separator)
            |> ignore

    // if list hasValues remove last separator
    if hasValues then
```

```
        result.Remove(result.Length - separator.Length, separator.
Length) |> ignore

    // get result
    result.ToString()
```

In this example, we used a string builder as a state where values were added together with a separator string. Once the list was iterated through, there was one trailing separator that needed to be removed before the result could be returned. This is of course true only if the sequence was nonempty.

This is how it could be written in an immutable way:

```
// F# implementation of String.Join
let rec join separator = function
    | [] -> ""
    | hd :: [] -> hd.ToString()
    | hd :: tl -> hd.ToString() + separator + (join separator tl)
```

This implementation is quite stupid, but it is proving the point of immutability. Instead of having a state that is mutated, we used recursion to apply the same method once again with different parameters. This is much easier to test, as there are no moving parts within the function. There is nothing to debug, as there is no state that is changing.

If one were to create an expressive solution to this problem, it would rather look like this:

```
// F# implementation of String.Join
let join separator =
    // use separator to separate two strings
    let _separate s1 s2 = s1 + separator + s2
    // reduce list using the separator helper function
    List.reduce _separate
```

In this implementation, we add a few constraints by narrowing down the specification. Only a list of strings are now allowed, and the implementation will throw a System.ArgumentException exception when it encounters an empty list. This is OK if it's a part of the specification.

The problem itself is a reduce problem, so it is natural to use the higher order reduce function to solve it. All of this was, of course, a matter of exercise. You should always use the built-in String.Join function and never roll your own.

This is where you can see the functional programming excel. We moved from a 20 **Lines of Code (LOC)** mutable code example to a 3 LOC immutable code example.

Less code makes it easier to test, and less code may also reduce the need for testing. Each line of code brings complexity, and if we can bring down the number of lines of code by writing terser code, we also reduce the need for testing.

Immutable data structures

As we have seen, the immutable value is default in F# compared to the mutable variable in other languages. But the statement that F# makes on immutability doesn't end here. The default way of creating types in F# makes for immutable types.

An immutable type is where you set values upon creation of an instance, and each attempt to modify the state of the instance will result in a new instance. The most comprehensive example in .NET is `DateTime`.

This makes it possible for us to use function chaining like this:

```
// Now + 1 year + 1 month + 1 day
> System.DateTime.Today.AddYears(1).AddMonths(1).AddDays(1.)
```

In F#, we define a new type like this:

```
> type Customer = { FirstName : string; Surname : string;
CreditCardNumber: string }
> let me = { FirstName = "Mikael"; Surname = "Lundin"; CreditCardNumber =
"1234567890" }
```

Now if I update the credit card number, it generates an new instance.

```
let meNext = { me with CreditCardNumber = "2345678901" }
```

There are many benefits of doing this:

- If you are processing the `me` parameter, it will not change its state, making `async` operations safe.
- All data that belongs to the `me` parameter is accurate at the point in time when the `me` parameter was created. If we change `me`, we lose this consistency.

Fewer moving parts also make it easier to test code, as we don't have to care about the state and can focus on the input and output of functions. When dealing with systems such as trading and online ordering, immutability has become such a major player that now there are immutable databases. Take a look at **Datomic** and validate how an immutable database fits into immutable code.

Built-in immutable types

In order to support immutability throughout the language, there are some immutable types that come with the F# framework. These support pretty much any kind of functional computation that you would need, and with them, you can compose your own immutable type.

Most of the already defined types and data structures within the .NET framework are mutable, and you should avoid them where you can and sometimes create your own immutable versions of the functionality. It is important to find a balance here between cost versus value.

Tuple

Tuple is one of the most common data types with the F# language and is simply a way of storing two or several values in one container.

The following code is an example of a tuple:

```
// pattern matching
let tuple = (1, 2)
let a, b = tuple
printfn "%d + %d = %d" a b (a + b)
```

A tuple is immutable because once it's created, you cannot change the values without creating a new tuple.

Another important aspect of the tuple is how it maps to the out keyword of C#. Where the .NET framework supports out variables, it will be translated into a tuple in F#. The most common usage of the out keyword is the Try pattern. as follows:

```
// instead of bool.TryParse
// s -> bool choice
let parseBool s =
    match bool.TryParse(s) with
    // success, value
    | true, b  -> Some(b)
    | false, _ -> None
```

The code maps the bool.TryParse functionality into the choice type. which becomes less prone to error as it forces you to handle the None case, and it only has three combinations of values instead of four, as with the tuple result.

This can be tested as follows:

```
[<Test>]
let ``should parse "true" as true`` () =
    parseBool "true" |> should equal (Some true)

[<Test>]
let ``should parse "false" as false`` () =
    parseBool "false" |> should equal (Some false)

[<Test>]
let ``cannot parse string gives none`` () =
    parseBool "FileNotFound" |> should equal None
```

List

The list type is a very used collection type throughout F#, and it has very little in common with its mutable cousin: the System.Collections.Generic.List<T> type. Instead, it is more like a linked list with a closer resemblance to **Lisp**.

The following image shows the working of lists:

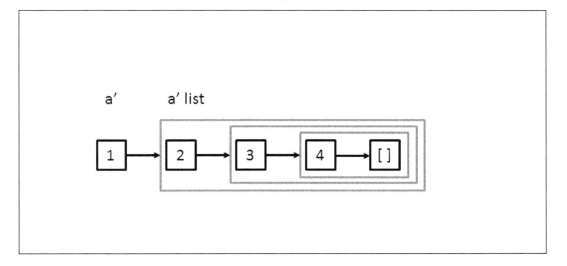

The immutable list of F# has the following properties:

- Head
- IsEmpty
- Item
- Length
- Tail

This is enough to perform most computations that require collections Here is an example of a common way to build lists with recursion:

```
// not very optimized way of getting factors of n
let factors n =
    let rec _factors = function
    | 1 -> [1]
    | k when n % k = 0 -> k :: _factors (k - 1)
    | k -> _factors (k - 1)

    _factors (n / 2)
```

One strength of the list type is the built-in language features:

```
// create a list
> [1..5];;
val it : int list = [1; 2; 3; 4; 5]

// pattern matching
let a :: b :: _ = [1..5];;
val b : int = 2
val a : int = 1

// generate list
> [for i in 1..5 -> i * i];;
val it : int list = [1; 4; 9; 16; 25]
```

Another strength of the list type is the list module and its higher order functions. I will give an example here of a few higher order functions that are very powerful to use together with the list type.

The map is a higher order function that will let you apply a function to each element in the list:

```
// map example
let double = (*) 2
```

```
let numbers = [1..5] |> List.map double

// val numbers : int list = [2; 4; 6; 8; 10]
```

The `fold` is a higher order function that will aggregate the `list` items with an accumulator value:

```
// fold example
let separateWithSpace = sprintf "%O %d"
let joined = [1..5] |> List.fold separateWithSpace "Joined:"

// val joined : string = "Joined: 1 2 3 4 5"
```

The nice thing about the `fold` function is that you can apply it to two lists as well. This is nice when you want to compute a value between two lists.

The following image is an example of this, using two lists of numbers. The algorithm described is called **Luhn** and is used to validate Swedish social security numbers. The result of this calculation should always be 0 for the **Social Security Number (SSN)** to be valid:

```
    1 9 3 8 0 8 2 0 9 0 0 5
  * 2 1 2 1 2 1 2 1 2 1 2 1
    2+9+6+8+0+8+4+0+18+0+0+5  =  60
                                 % 10
                                  0
```

Here is a perfect situation where you want to compute a value between two lists:

```
// fold2 example
let multiplier = [for i in [1..12] -> (i % 2) + 1] // 2; 1; 2; 1...
let multiply acc a b = acc + (a * b)
let luhn ssn = (List.fold2 multiply 0 ssn multiplier) % 10

let result = luhn [1; 9; 3; 8; 0; 8; 2; 0; 9; 0; 0; 5]

// val result : int = 0
```

The partition is an excellent higher order function to use when you need to split values in a list into separate lists:

```
// partition example
let overSixteen = fun x -> x > 16
let youthPartition = [10..23] |> List.partition overSixteen

// val youthPartition : int list * int list =
//    ([17; 18; 19; 20; 21; 22; 23], [10; 11; 12; 13; 14; 15; 16])
```

The reduce is a higher order function that will not use an accumulator value through the aggregation like the fold function, but uses the computation of the first two values as a seed.

The following code shows the reduce function:

```
// reduce example
let lesser a b = if a < b then a else b
let min = [6; 34; 2; 75; 23] |> List.reduce lesser
```

There are many more useful higher order functions in the List module that are free for you to explore.

Sequence

Sequence in F# is the implementation of the .NET framework's IEnumerable interface. It lets you get one element at a time without any other information about the sequence. There is no knowledge about the size of the sequence.

The F# sequence is strongly typed and quite powerful when combined with the seq computational expression. It will let us create unlimited length lists just like the yield keyword in C#:

```
// For multiples of three print "Fizz" instead of the number
// and for multiples of five print "Buzz"
// for multiples of both write "Fizzbuzz"
let fizzbuzz =
    let rec _fizzbuzz n =
        seq {
            match n with
            | n when n % 15 = 0 -> yield "Fizzbuzz"
            | n when n % 3 = 0  -> yield "Fizz"
            | n when n % 5 = 0 -> yield "Buzz"
            | n -> yield n.ToString()

            yield! _fizzbuzz (n + 1)
```

```
        }

    _fizzbuzz 1
```

I'm sure you recognize the classic recruitment test. This code will generate an infinite sequence of `fizzbuzz` output for as long as a new value is requested.

The test for this algorithm clearly shows the usage of sequences:

```
[<Test>]
let ``should verify the first 15 computations of the fizzbuzz
sequence`` () =
    fizzbuzz
        |> Seq.take 15
        |> Seq.reduce (sprintf "%s %s")
        |> should equal "1 2 Fizz 4 Buzz Fizz 7 8 Fizz Buzz 11 Fizz 13
14 Fizzbuzz"
```

Creating an immutable type

When you set out to create your own types, you have great tools that will help you start out with immutable versions. The most basic type declaration is the discriminated union:

```
// xml representation
type Node =
    | Attribute of string * string
    | Element of Node list
    | Value of string
```

A basic type is that of a record, which is in its basic setting an immutable type:

```
let quote =
    Element
        [
            Attribute ("cite", "Alan Turing")
            Value "Machines take me by surprise with great frequency"
        ]
```

In order to change the value of an immutable type, you need to create a new copy of it with the value changed, a true immutable type:

```
// <blockquote cite="Alan Turing">Machines take me by surprise with
great frequency</blockquote>
```

Once in a while, you need to create a class, and this is when you need to be careful to create an immutable type and not a mutable one. This can be identified by the following properties:

- State can only be set upon creation
- Change of state returns a copy of the instance
- The class can only have references to other immutable types

This is an example of a good immutable class type:

```
type Vector = | X | Y | Z

type Point(x : int, y : int, z : int) =

    // read-only properties
    member __.X = x
    member __.Y = y
    member __.Z = z

    // update
    member this.Update value = function
    | X -> Point(value, y, z)
    | Y -> Point(x, value, z)
    | Z -> Point(x, y, value)

    override this.Equals (obj) =
        match obj with
        | :? Point as p -> p.X = this.X && p.Y = this.Y && p.Z =
this.Z
        | _ -> false

    override this.ToString () = sprintf "{%d, %d, %d}" x y z
```

When updating any value, it will generate a new instance of `Point` instead of mutating the existing one, which makes for a good immutable class.

Writing testable code

In the previous section we have been looking at basic functional structures that helps us write better programs. Now we're ready to move on to higher level constructs that let us organize our code functionally on a more abstract way.

Active patterns

Pattern matching is one of the killer features of F# that makes it a more attractive language than C# or Visual Basic. It could have been just a nice language feature for the built-in .NET types, but actually it is highly customizable and you can define your own patterns.

Here is how you can define your own active pattern:

```
// active pattern for sequences
let (|Empty|NotEmpty|) sequence =
    if Seq.isEmpty sequence then Empty
    else NotEmpty sequence
```

This enables us to use the pattern directly in a match expression:

```
// example on usage of active pattern
// join ["1"; "2"; "3"] -> "123"
let rec join (s : seq<string>) =
    match s with
    | Empty -> ""
    | NotEmpty s -> (Seq.head s) + join (Seq.skip 1 s)
```

The power of this really comes into play when using parameterized active patterns together with a complex concept, such as regular expressions:

```
// matching input to pattern and return matching values
let (|Matches|) (pattern : string) (input : string) =
    let matches = Regex.Matches(input, pattern)
    [for m in matches -> m.Value]
```

This pattern will match a string and run a regular expression pattern on it, returning the values of the matches. This makes for a nice combination of regular expressions and pattern matching:

```
// parse a serial key and concat the parts
let parseSerialKey = function
| Matches @"\w{5}" values -> System.String.Join("", values)
```

Here is an example of how to execute this function:

```
> parseSerialKey "VP9VV-VJW7Q-MHY6W-JK47R-M2KGJ";;
val it : string = "VP9VVVJW7QMHY6WJK47RM2KGJ"
```

This language feature makes it easier to separate out the ceremonial code to run a regular expression and the actual expression that is part of the business logic. It also makes for very readable code.

Higher order functions

We have seen examples of higher order functions for the `list` data structure. One easy thing to gain testability in functional programming is to write your own higher order functions and use the structure to gain higher cohesion and easier-to-test functions in isolation:

```
// get url content and transform it
let webGet transformer urls =
    let _download url =
        let webClient = new WebClient()

        try
            let uri = new System.Uri(url)
            webClient.DownloadString(uri)

        finally
            webClient.Dispose()

    List.map (_download >> transformer) urls
```

This is a higher order function that will download URLs and accept a function for what to do with the content of those URLs. This way, we can easily isolate the testing of downloading the contents of a URL, which naturally becomes an integration test, and the transformation of the result, which might or might not be a perfect unit test.

Partial application

One very simple way of dealing with dependencies in functional application is by using partial application.

Partial application will assume an unknown argument and return a function that requires one or several arguments in order to be completed. A simple way is to consider partial application when dealing with databases:

```
type PaymentStatus = | Unpaid | Paid | Overpaid | PartlyPaid
type Order = { id : string; paymentStatus : PaymentStatus }

// interface that describes the function to persist an order
type IPersistOrder =
    abstract member Save: Order -> Order

// update payment status in database

let updatePaymentStatus order status =
    (fun (dataAccess : IPersistOrder) ->
        let newOrder = { order with paymentStatus = status }
        dataAccess.Save(newOrder)
    )
```

The updatePaymentStatus function has a dependency on an IPersistOrder
parameter. It could easily take this dependency as another argument, but instead,
we chose to make the dependency obvious to the reader by returning a function.

What we can now do in our tests is replace the IPersistOrder parameter with a
stub implementation, as follows:

```
type StubPersistOrder () =
    interface IPersistOrder with
        member this.Save m = m

[<Test>]
let ''should save an order with updated status'' () =
    // setup
    let order = { id = "12890"; paymentStatus = Unpaid}
    let orderDA = new StubPersistOrder()

    // test
    let persistedOrder = updatePaymentStatus order Paid orderDA

    // assert
    persistedOrder.paymentStatus |> should equal Paid
```

This method of replacing dependencies with interfaces takes on an object-oriented
approach. In a functional language, we could easily replace the interface with a
function definition instead and achieve the same result:

```
type PaymentStatus = | Unpaid | Paid | Overpaid | PartlyPaid
type Order = { id : string; paymentStatus : PaymentStatus }

// update payment status in database

let updatePaymentStatus order status =
    (fun (save : Order -> Order)  ->
        let newOrder = { order with paymentStatus = status }
        save newOrder
    )
```

The test for this can also be simplified. We no longer need an instantiation of an interface:

```
[<Test>]
let ``should save an order with updated status`` () =
    // setup
    let order = { id = "12890"; paymentStatus = Unpaid}
    let nothing = (fun arg -> arg)

    // test
    let persistedOrder = updatePaymentStatus order Paid nothing

    // assert
    persistedOrder.paymentStatus |> should equal Paid
```

The problem with using partial application for dependency injection is that it fast becomes the same mess as you have with dependency injection in an object-oriented program. You have a dependency tree that becomes extremely deep, and you will have problems creating any kind of business object without creating a whole universe around it.

The following image is a simplification of the object dependency graph we had for one of the entities in a system that I worked on for a client:

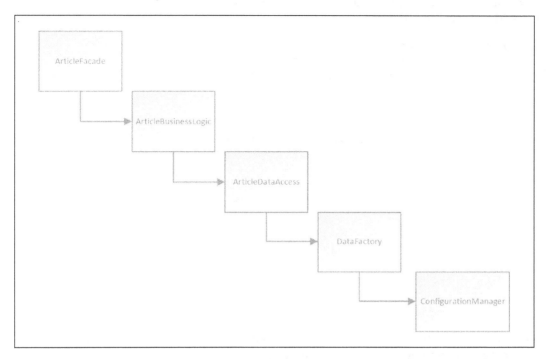

The effect is that you can't create a simple object without including all of its dependencies, and every time you need to do something, you also need to create all of these dependencies. This is where dependency injection frameworks come from to solve this kind of problem, but it really is just a band aid on top of a larger code smell.

Continuations

Let's say that I want to write a function that will get all links on a certain web page. Consider the following implementation:

```
// get string from url, pass result to success() or failure()
let webget_bad (url : string) success failure =
    let client = new System.Net.WebClient()

    try
        try
            // get content from web request
            let content = client.DownloadString(url)

            // match all href attributes in html code
            let matches = Regex.Matches(content, "href=\"(.+?)\"")

            // get all matching groups
            [for m in matches -> m.Groups.[1].Value]
        with
            | ex -> failure(ex)
    finally
        client.Dispose()
```

This is very hard to test because the function itself is doing several things, such as web requests and parsing HTML attributes.

Continuation is the method of abstracting away the next step of a computation. This can be very useful when you want to create a generic function without specifying what will happen with the result.

The easiest example is that of a web client call:

```
// get string from url, pass result to success() or failure()
let webget (url : string) success failure =
    let client = new System.Net.WebClient()

    try
        try
            let content = client.DownloadString(url)
            success(content)
        with
```

```
        | ex -> failure(ex)
    finally
        client.Dispose()
```

What we have here is a method with a nasty side effect of doing a web client call. This has to be wrapped not only in a `try..finally` clause but also in `try..with` for error management.

Success and failure are our continuations that enable us to separate out the pure functionality from the impure. This makes the code in success and failure very easy to test apart form the web client call:

```
// success: parse links from html
let parseLinks html =
    let matches = Regex.Matches(html, "href=\"(.+?)\"")
    [for m in matches -> m.Groups.[1].Value]

// failure: print exception message and return empty list
let printExceptionMessage (ex : System.Exception) =
    printfn "Failed: %s" ex.Message; []
```

The trade-off you make using continuations is a more explicit function declaration with more arguments. This doesn't mean that you lose readability if you extract those methods and name them properly:

```
> webget "http://blog.mikaellundin.name" parseLinks printExceptionMessage
```

The following image shows the preceding command-line output:

```
F# Interactive                                                              ▾ ☐ ✕
> webget "http://blog.mikaellundin.name" parseLinks printExceptionMessage;;
val it : string list =
  ["http://blog.mikaellundin.name/res/screen.css";
   "http://blog.mikaellundin.name/res/print.css";
   "http://blog.mikaellundin.name/feed.xml";
   "http://blog.mikaellundin.name/assets/css/font-awesome.min.css";
   "http://blog.mikaellundin.name/assets/css/pygments-jekyll-github.css";
   "http://blog.mikaellundin.name"; "http://blog.mikaellundin.name/archive/";
   "http://blog.mikaellundin.name/feed.xml";
   "http://blog.mikaellundin.name/about/"; "//mikaellundin.name";
   "//twitter.com/mikaellundin"; "//github.com/miklund/tailcalloptimized";
   "/2014/08/31/how-to-fix-your-sony-pulse-headset.html";
   "/2014/05/02/tdd-is-not-dead.html"; "/2014/04/25/bugs-and-defects.html";
   "/2014/04/02/my-view-on-project-management.html";
   "/2014/03/24/tail-call-optimization.html"; "/archive/"]
```

The code shows that something that is quite hard to extract into testable code in an imperative programming language, where one would inject object instances, is very easy to do with continuations in F# and achieve in very few lines of code.

Expressiveness through functional programming

There is a very important distinction between programming language paradigms. Two kinds of programming styles stand against each other:

- Imperative programming
- Declarative programming

The imperative programming style has its origin in Fortran, and the declarative programming paradigm's roots can be followed back to Lisp. The following sections will compare the two styles and explain why we prefer one over the other in testing.

Imperative programming

Imperative programming has become the standard of programming methodology with the rise of languages such as BASIC, Pascal, C, and C#. It means describing to the computer how to calculate a result, in a way that you would describe how to make a cake:

```
// imperative programming
let double_imperative numbers =
    let doubled = System.Collections.Generic.List<int>()

    for number in numbers do
        let double = number * 2
        doubled.Add(double)

    doubled
```

This code example will double all the values in a list by first creating a result list and then doubling it number by number and adding it to the result. Once it goes through all the numbers, the result list will be returned.

In this code, there is a clear path of how double values are calculated, and the program describes how this is accomplished.

Declarative programming

Instead of instructing the computer how to calculate a result, you can describe what the result is. If the result is too complex, break it down into parts and describe the parts and then concatenate those parts. It leads you to a series of descriptions instead of a workflow of what should be done:

```
// declarative programming
let double numbers =
    let double = (*) 2
    Seq.map double numbers
```

This code example also doubles all the values in a list, but instead of describing how this is done, the code describes what this means:

- The `double` function means taking a value and multiplying it by 2
- Result implies by mapping `double` onto the `numbers` function

The main difference between these two methods is that imperative programming describes how and declarative programming describes what. The imperative example created a state to bake the cake, whereas the declarative example broke down the problem into describable parts.

Declarative programming is less prone to faults because there is no mutable state. It is also easier to test as you break down the problem into isolated parts that are not only individually describable but also individually testable. This way, there is a high increase in quality and testability when you use declarative programming.

Let's look at another example. You need to parse roman numerals into integers. In an imperative programming style, you would go about doing this in the following manner:

```
// parse a roman numeral and return its value
let parse (s : string) =
    // mutable value
    let mutable input = s
    let mutable result = 0

    let romanNumerals =
        [|("M",1000); ("CM" ,900); ("D",500); ("CD",400); ("C",100 );
        ("XC",90); ("L",50); ("XL",40); ("X",10 ); ("IX",9); ("V",5);
        ("IV",4); ("I", 1)|]

    while not (String.IsNullOrEmpty input) do
        let mutable found = false
        let mutable i = 0

        // iterate over romanNumerals matching it with input string
        while (not found) || i < romanNumerals.Length do
            let romanNumeral, value = romanNumerals.[i]

            // does input start with current romanNumeral?
```

```
            if input.StartsWith(romanNumeral, StringComparison.
CurrentCultureIgnoreCase) then
                result <- result + value
                input <- input.Substring(romanNumeral.Length)
                found <- true

            // iterate
            i <- i + 1

        // no roman numeral found at beginning of string
        if (not found) then
            failwith "invalid roman numeral"

    result
```

The following is the basic usage of the parse function:

```
> parse "MMXIV";;
val it : int = 2014
```

The code starts by creating two mutable variables: one is a working copy of the incoming value and the other is a result variable. The program will then work on the input variable, matching the start of the string with roman numerals and as a numeral is found adding its value to the result and removing it from the input string. Once the string is empty, the parsing is complete and the value is in the result variable.

There are a lot of moving parts in this code, and it is hard to debug because of the different states that the variables can be in.

Here's an example of how to write this in a more expressive and declarative way:

```
// partial active pattern to match start of string
let (|StartsWith|_|) (p : string) (s : string) =
    if s.StartsWith(p, StringComparison.CurrentCultureIgnoreCase) then
        Some(s.Substring(p.Length))
    else
        None

// parse a roman numeral and return its value
let rec parse = function
| "" -> 0
| StartsWith "M" rest  -> 1000 + (parse rest)
| StartsWith "CM" rest -> 900 + (parse rest)
| StartsWith "D" rest  -> 500 + (parse rest)
| StartsWith "CD" rest -> 400 + (parse rest)
| StartsWith "C" rest  -> 100 + (parse rest)
```

```
| StartsWith "XC" rest -> 90 + (parse rest)
| StartsWith "L" rest  -> 50 + (parse rest)
| StartsWith "XL" rest -> 40 + (parse rest)
| StartsWith "X" rest  -> 10 + (parse rest)
| StartsWith "IX" rest -> 9 + (parse rest)
| StartsWith "V" rest  -> 5 + (parse rest)
| StartsWith "IV" rest -> 4 + (parse rest)
| StartsWith "I" rest  -> 1 + (parse rest)
| _ -> failwith "invalid roman numeral"
```

The following is the basic usage of the function:

```
> parse "MMXIV";;
val it : int = 2014
```

This code used an F# concept called active pattern and then used pattern matching to match the beginning of the string with the different roman numerals. The value of the parsed numeral is added by parsing the rest of the string.

There are no moving parts in this example, only expressions of what each Roman numeral is worth. The functionality is easier to debug and to test.

Tail call optimization

Writing expressive code is very powerful and gives your code a lot of readability, but it can also be hurtful.

The following will create a comma-separated string out of a list of values:

```
// join values together to a comma separated string
let rec join = function
| [] -> ""
| hd :: [] -> hd
| hd :: tl -> hd + ", " + (join tl)
```

This code will expand into the following call tree.

```
> ["1"; "2"; "3"; "4"; "5"] |> join;;
join ["1"; "2"; "3"; "4"; "5"]
<- join ["2"; "3"; "4"; "5"]
  <- join ["3"; "4"; "5"]
    <- join ["4"; "5"]
      <- join ["5"]
        <- join []
```

There are two problems with this:

- It is very inefficient to perform these many function calls
- Each function call will occupy a record on the stack, leading to stack overflow for large recursion trees

We can show this by running the following tests. First, we run the `join` function with 30,000 items with timing on:

```
> #time;;

> [1..30000] |> List.map (fun n -> n.ToString()) |> join;;
Real: 00:00:06.288, CPU: 00:00:06.203, GC gen0: 140, gen1: 61, gen2: 60
val it : string = "1, 2, .... 30000"
```

The execution lasts for about 6 seconds. In the second test, we run the `join` function with 1,00,000 items:

```
> [1..100000] |> List.map (fun n -> n.ToString()) |> join;;
Process is terminated due to StackOverflowException.
Session termination detected. Press Enter to restart.
```

The result is a crash because there was not enough room on the stack for that many items.

The F# compiler has something called tail call optimization to deal with these problems. You can write expressive code and still have it running safe without the risk of the StackOverflowException exception. You only need to be aware of how to write code so it becomes optimized:

```
// join values together to a comma separated string
let join list =
    let rec _join res = function
    | [] -> res
    | hd :: tl -> _join (res + ", " + hd) tl

    if list = List.Empty then
        ""
    else
        (_join (List.head list) (List.tail list))
```

The structure of this function is somewhat different. Instead of returning the result, the result is built up into a result argument for each recursion. The fact that the recursive call is the last call of the function makes it possible for the compiler to optimize it.

I'm using an inner function `join` because of two reasons. First, to avoid exposing the `res` argument to the caller, as it should not be a part of the function definition.

The other is to simplify the match case, as the first iteration should only add the head element of the list to the result.

We can write a test to make sure that it can handle a lot of items:

```
[<Test>]
let ``should be able to handle 100000 items`` () =
    let values = [1..100000] |> List.map (fun n -> n.ToString())
    (fun () -> (join values) |> ignore) |> should not' (throw
typeof<System.StackOverflowException>)
```

This gives us an idea of whether the function is able to handle the amount of data we're expecting to throw at it, but it really doesn't say whether it will eventually overflow the stack.

You can use a tool such as **ilspy** to decompile the assemblies and look at the **Intermediate Language** (**IL**) code. Let's take a look at what our first example looks like in C# after decompiling it:

```
public static string join(FSharpList<string> _arg1)
{
  if (_arg1.TailOrNull == null)
  {
    return "";
  }
  if (_arg1.TailOrNull.TailOrNull == null)
  {
    return _arg1.HeadOrDefault;
  }
  FSharpList<string> tl = _arg1.TailOrNull;
  string hd = _arg1.HeadOrDefault;
  return hd + ", " + _12320S_04_08.join(tl);
}
```

The last line is the culprit where the method makes a call to itself. Now, let's look at the second example with the tail recursion optimization:

```
public static string join(FSharpList<string> list)
{
  FSharpFunc<string, FSharpFunc<FSharpList<string>, string>> _join =
new _12320S_04_09._join@7();
  return FSharpFunc<string, FSharpList<string>>.InvokeFast<string>(_
join, ListModule.Head<string>(list), ListModule.Tail<string>(list));
```

```
    }

    [Serializable]
    internal class _join@7 : OptimizedClosures.FSharpFunc<string,
    FSharpList<string>, string>
    {
      internal _join@7()
      {
      }
      public override string Invoke(string res, FSharpList<string> _arg1)
      {
        while (true)
        {
          FSharpList<string> fSharpList = _arg1;
          if (fSharpList.TailOrNull == null)
          {
            break;
          }
          FSharpList<string> fSharpList2 = fSharpList;
          FSharpList<string> tl = fSharpList2.TailOrNull;
          string hd = fSharpList2.HeadOrDefault;
          string arg_33_0 = res + ", " + hd;
          _arg1 = tl;
          res = arg_33_0;
        }
        return res;
      }
    }
```

F# is not very beautiful anymore after it got decompiled to C#, but the message here is clear. In the second example, the compiler optimized the recursive call into a while(true) loop, and this solved the whole problem with the stack overflow.

When writing expressive, declarative code, it is important to understand tail recursion. It is one of those things that will bite you, not while writing the code but in production where the data is much more diverse and hard to predict.

It is important to understand when to strive for tail call optimization and how to verify that it's actually there.

Parallel execution

The following was quoted in 2005:

"The free lunch is over."

– Herb Sutter

Since this happened, we have been looking for a way to do parallel execution in a simple way. Our computers aren't getting faster, but they are gaining more and more parallel execution power. This is, however, useless unless we find a way of utilizing this power.

We struggle to make our applications scale out to several CPU cores. Our tools have threads, locks, mutexes, and semaphores, and still we're not able to write concurrent programs that work well. This is because using those tools is very hard. Predicting the execution flow in a concurrent program is very hard and so is debugging a concurrent program.

The result of threading and locks leads to problems such as race conditions and deadlocks. One of the major caveats for concurrent programming is the state, and a mutable state is the beloved best friend of imperative programming. There is a major difference in parallelizing the imperative and declarative programs.

You have two reasons for your application to become concurrent:

- Your program is CPU-bound
- Your program is I/O-bound

For this purpose, F# has the `async` computational expression:

```
// download contents to url
let download url =
    printfn "Start: %s" url
    async {
        // create client
        let webClient = new WebClient()

        try
            let uri = System.Uri(url)

            // download string
            return! webClient.AsyncDownloadString(uri)

        finally
```

```
                          printfn "Finish: %s" url
                          webClient.Dispose()
            }
```

We can quite easily provide a test for this code if we are aware of the consequences of its side effects:

```
[<Test>]
let ``should download three urls in parallel`` () =
    let baseUrl = "http://blog.mikaellundin.name"
    let paths = [
        "/2014/08/31/how-to-fix-your-sony-pulse-headset.html";
        "/2014/05/02/tdd-is-not-dead.html";
        "/2014/04/25/bugs-and-defects.html"]

    // build urls
    let urls = paths |> List.map (fun path -> baseUrl + path)

    // test & await
    let result = urls |> List.map (download) |> Async.Parallel |>
Async.RunSynchronously

    // assert
    Assert.That((result |> (Seq.nth 0)), Is.StringContaining "Sony
Pulse Headset")
    Assert.That((result |> (Seq.nth 1)), Is.StringContaining "Writing
code is not easy")
    Assert.That((result |> (Seq.nth 2)), Is.StringContaining "Lexical
Errors")
```

The important aspect here is that execution of individual computations don't need to end in the same order as they begin, but they will still render the same result.

This can be seen in the test output, as follows.

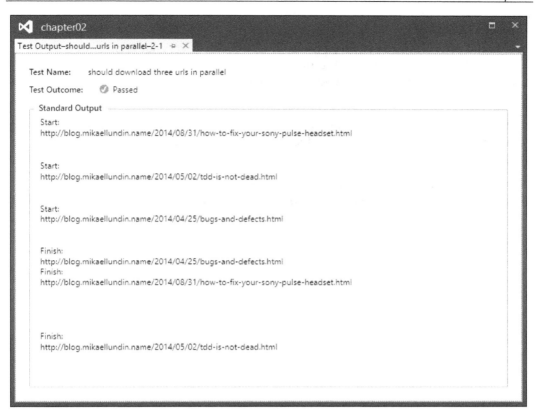

Writing code that is without side effects can help when you need to do concurrent programming because it will simplify the scenarios of having no state and needing no lock mechanisms. The declarative way of writing asynchronous code in F# makes it easier to test, as parallelization can be isolated within a function member and tested from a black box perspective.

Summary

Functional programming is very powerful as it leads to very terse programs with high-quality and low number of faults. This is because good functional code doesn't have any side effects — a place where most of the imperative object-oriented code has its bugs.

In this chapter, we've been looking at functional concepts that make it easier to write good code that doesn't cause side effects and has a low number of bugs, but also code that is easier to test.

The next chapter we'll reach into the toolset that exists for programs written in F# and what it takes to get started with functional testing.

3
Setting Up Your Test Environment

Before getting started with writing unit tests, we need to make sure we have an environment good enough for running them. There are some tools built into Visual Studio we will use for development: tools to download and tools to buy.

This chapter will be a step-to-step guide on how to set up your test environment by covering the following subjects:

- F# Interactive
- Testing in Visual Studio
- Testing outside Visual Studio
- Setting up a build script with **FAKE (F# Make)**
- Running tests in continuous integration

After reading this chapter, you will be ready to start writing tests.

F# Interactive

One of the coolest things about F# is that its development environment comes with an interactive test environment: F# Interactive. You can access this feature in Visual Studio's top menu by navigating to **View | Other Windows | F# Interactive** or pressing the default shortcut *Ctrl + Alt + F*, as shown in the following screenshot:

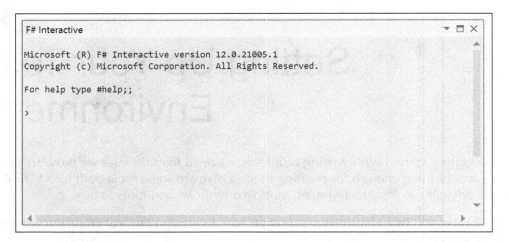

This is valuable when we need to do the following:

- Quickly validate computations
- Spike new concepts
- Validate the implemented solution

When working with F#, you can use the interactive window to quickly validate part of a solution before implementing it. It provides a kind of a workbench when developing a test environment.

Let's say you need to implement a function that checks whether the current year is a leap year. You can enter the following code into F# Interactive in order to understand how the .NET framework manages to create a date that is not valid:

```
> new System.DateTime(System.DateTime.Today.Year, 2, 29);;

System.ArgumentOutOfRangeException: Year, Month, and Day parameters
describe an un-representable DateTime.

   at System.DateTime.DateToTicks(Int32 year, Int32 month, Int32 day)

   at <StartupCode$FSI_0004>.$FSI_0004.main@()

Stopped due to error
```

Working with F# Interactive, we end each statement with ;; in order to tell the interpreter that it should validate. That way we can enter several lines of code without having it run until we send ;; to F# Interactive.

This tells us that we can expect an `ArgumentOutOfRangeException` exception when we enter a date that is not valid. So, let's use this in our routine to find leap years:

```
open System

// is the year a leap year?
let isLeapYear year =
    try
        let date = DateTime(year, 2, 29)
        true
    with
        | :? ArgumentOutOfRangeException -> false
```

Now, we can use F# Interactive to validate this function. We will do this by writing the code in new F# code file. Select the code and press *Alt + Enter* or right-click and select **Execute in Interactive**.

You will get the following output in the F# Interactive window:

val isLeapYear : year : int -> bool

Now, you can validate that the code is doing what you as a programmer expected it to do by interactively testing it from the interactive prompt:

> [2000..2014] |> List.filter isLeapYear ;;
val it : int list = [2000; 2004; 2008; 2012]

In most other languages, you can't test the written code before it has been compiled into a runnable state; however, in F#, you can grab parts of the implemented solution and test it interactively. This leads to you spending less time on debugging and features that only work the first time you run them.

Loading external references

Once your application starts to grow, you will need to perform more advanced actions in F# Interactive that will require you to load external libraries. The interactive shell cannot resolve references automatically, but rather, needs some help.

Let's say we include the `Newtonsoft.Json` library to be able to quickly turn our F# types into JSON, and we want to test this in F# Interactive:

```
open Newtonsoft.Json
let toJson = JsonConvert.SerializeObject
```

We will get the following error message when trying to execute the preceding lines in the interactive shell:

```
1232OS_05_02.fs(5,10): error FS0039: The namespace or module 'Newtonsoft'
is not defined
```

In order to get the path to the library you want to reference, right-click on **References** in the **Solution Explorer** tab and copy the **Full Path** property value, as shown in the following screenshot:

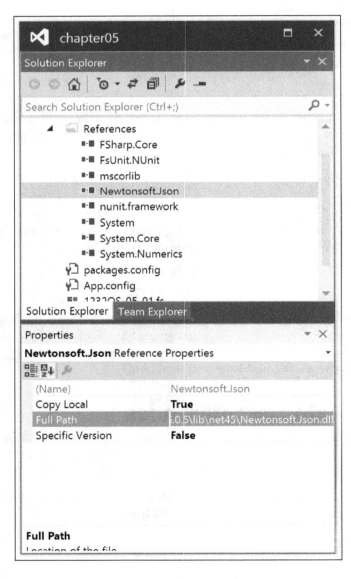

The interactive shell doesn't have the solution directory as its current working directory, so we need to specify the absolute paths to the assemblies we want to reference:

```
> #I @"D:\code\packages\Newtonsoft.Json.6.0.5\lib\net45";;
```

```
--> Added 'D:\code\packages\Newtonsoft.Json.6.0.5\lib\net45' to library
include path
```

```
> #r Newtonsoft.Json";;
```

```
--> Referenced 'D:\code\packages\Newtonsoft.Json.6.0.5\lib\net45\
Newtonsoft.Json.dll' (file may be locked by F# Interactive process)
```

First, we'll add the installation path of the `Newtonsoft` library to the default assembly search path and then reference it by name.

Of course, when you have a large project, you don't want to include all your references manually. What you need to do then is create an `include` script in your F# application and reference that:

```
// add include paths
#I @".\packages\Newtonsoft.Json.6.0.5\lib\net45";;
// ... following more paths


// reference assemblies
#r @"Newtonsoft.Json";;
// ... following more references
```

In the `include` script, you can specify the paths that are relative to the script execution path, allowing the script to work with all developer machines and not just your own:

```
> #load @"D:\code\include.fsx";;
[Loading D:\code\include.fsx]


namespace FSI_0002
```

Now, you can use code that references types and modules within the external assemblies directly from F# Interactive.

Testing with Visual Studio

So far, we've been talking about interactive testing with F#. This is a basic concept in starting to write qualitative code, but what this book really is about is test automation.

Visual Studio Professional comes with some basic testing tools you can use to automate testing in your solution. They are, however, not made to work with F# and need some fiddling before you could begin using them, as explained in the following steps:

1. Create a new F# library project:

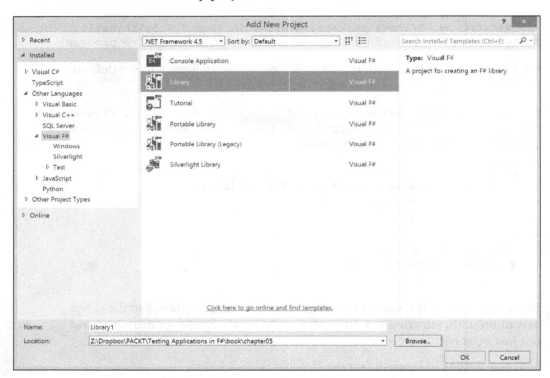

2. Add a reference to **Microsoft.VisualStudio.QualityTools. UnitTestingFramework**. This will later be referred to as MSTest:

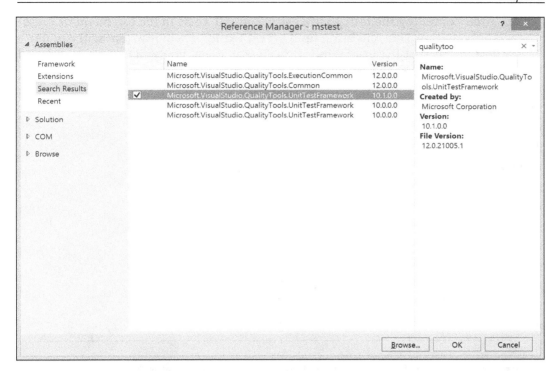

3. Create a new F# source file in your project with the `fs` extension. Now, you can write your first test, as follows:

```
module MSTest

open Microsoft.VisualStudio.TestTools.UnitTesting

[<TestClass>]
type CalculatorShould () =

    [<TestMethod>]
    member this.``add 1 and 2 with result of 3`` () =
        Assert.AreEqual(3, 1 + 2)
```

4. After compiling the test, go to **Test | Run All Tests** in the top menu or press *CTRL + R, A*. This will bring up the **Test Explorer** window that will run the test. If the **Test Explorer** window is already open, you will have to switch your focus to it in order to see the test results:

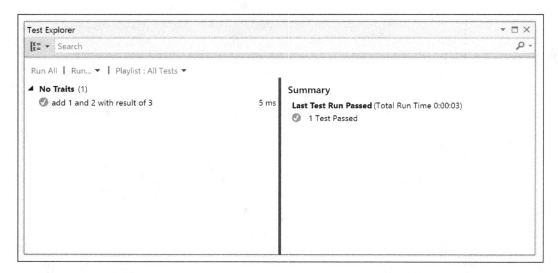

Congratulations! You have written and run your first automated test within Visual Studio.

NUnit

MSTest is not the optimal test framework. Actually, I consider it just slightly more convenient than using no test framework at all. Instead, the test framework considered as standard today is NUnit. This is why we'll take a look at how to get NUnit running within Visual Studio with F#:

1. First, you need to add the NUnit Test Adapter extension. Go to **Tools | Extensions and Updates** in the top menu bar and search for **nunit** in **Visual Studio Gallery**:

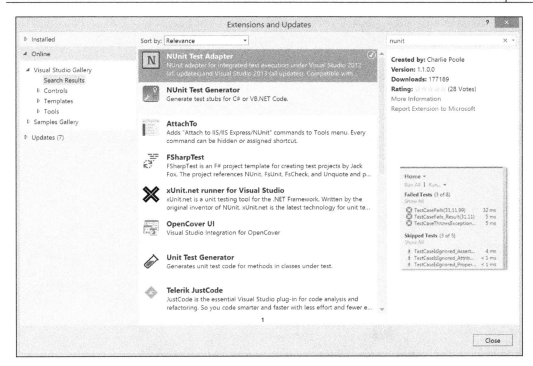

This adapter will make it possible to use the built-in Visual Studio test runner to execute NUnit tests.

2. Create a new F# library project and add NUnit.Framework as a reference to it through the **NuGet Package Manager**:

3. Now, we can write a unit test featuring **NUnit**:

```
module NUnitTests

open NUnit.Framework

[<Test>]
let ``calculator should add 1 and 2 with result of 3`` () =
    Assert.That(3, Is.EqualTo(1 + 2))
```

4. You can execute tests written with NUnit the same way you would execute with MSTest. After compiling the test, go to **Test | Run All Tests** in the top menu or press *CTRL + R, A*.

The main difference between tests written in MSTest and NUnit is that NUnit tests don't need a test class attribute. It is enough to mark out test methods that make the test procedure much simpler, as we can use the `let` statement for the tests, as well.

xUnit

While NUnit is a great replacement for MSTest, it still has a problem not being actively updated with new features, and the NUnit framework is very hard to extend. This is the major caveat of NUnit and the major issue xUnit is currently working to solve.

In order to run xUnit tests inside Visual Studio you need to add a NuGet package to your solution that contains the Visual Studio Test Adapter:

1. Right click on your solution in **Solution Explorer** and choose **Manage NuGet Packages for Solution**:

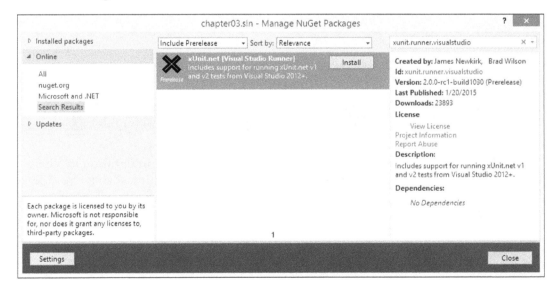

2. In the drop down box saying **Stable Only** you need to change it to **Include Prerelease**.
3. Search for **xunit.runner.visualstudio** and install the package to your solution.

4. Create a new F# library project and use the package manager to add **xUnit. net** to the current project:

5. Now, we can write a simple test to verify that the xUnit integration in Visual Studio works. The **Test Explorer** tab will pick up our unit test so we're able to execute it:

```
module 1232OS_05_06

open Xunit

[<Fact>]
let ``calculator should add 1 and 2 with result of 3`` () =
    Assert.Equal(3, 1 + 2)
```

6. The xUnit framework doesn't require class fixtures; we're just happy to attribute simple `let` functions as our tests.

Comparing MSTest, NUnit, and xUnit

We have just taken a look at how to get started with the three different testing frameworks: MSTest, NUnit, and xUnit. How should we choose between the three?

None of these frameworks are particularly designed to work with F# or functional programming, but they apply pretty well. MSTest is a bit cumbersome, as it requires a class with the `TestClass` attribute in order to execute the test suite.

The following highlights the strengths of the frameworks:

- **MSTest**: This is a good choice if you're not allowed to run open source in your organization.

- **NUnit**: This provides great support for external test data. It is the most mature open source test framework.

- **xUnit**: This is the best test framework when it comes to extensibility.

I would choose MSTest for organizations that have extremely high requirements on what kind of software you bring into a project. These could be pharmaceutical companies or those in the financial sector, in situations where compliance is more important than efficiency.

NUnit is the most frequently used testing framework in .NET and most likely the best choice when it comes to stability and widespread support. If you're writing code that will be shared outside the company or you want as little friction as possible in your continuous integration setup, you should select NUnit.

NUnit is a challenge when it comes to extensibility, however, and if you need to do something with your test suite that is not completely standard, you should select xUnit instead. It comes with an extensibility story and is easier to modify to suit your specific needs.

Tools and frameworks

The built-in tools for unit testing in Visual Studio are not the greatest. To smoothen the process, you need to use some external frameworks and tools.

FsUnit

The tests in this book will mainly focus on FsUnit as the main tool to write unit tests. This is not a test framework like NUnit or xUnit, but more of a helper library to write tests in a more functionally idiomatic way.

Let's start with an example. This function will get the date and time for the Swedish Midsummer in a specified year:

```
// find date of midsummer eve in Sweden
let midsummerEve year =
    // get a day in June
    let dateInJune day = new System.DateTime(year, 6, day)
    // is specified date a friday
    let isFriday (date : System.DateTime) = date.DayOfWeek = System.
DayOfWeek.Friday
    // find first friday between 19-26 june
    [19..26] |> List.map dateInJune |> List.find isFriday
```

Instead of writing a test like this:

```
open NUnit.Framework

// testing using NUnit
[<Test>]
let ``midsummer eve in 2014 should occur Jun 20`` () =
    // test
    let result = midsummerEve 2014

    // assert
    Assert.That(result.ToString("MMM d"), Is.EqualTo("Jun 20"))
```

You can instead write it with FsUnit, like this:

```
open NUnit.Framework
open FsUnit

// testing using fsunit
[<Test>]
let ``midsummer eve in 2014 should occur Jun 19`` () =
    (midsummerEve 2015).ToString("MMM d") |> should equal "Jun 19"
```

The FsUnit way of writing the assertion is a bit more terse and functional. This is why it is preferred.

Start by adding **FsUnit** as a NuGet package to your project, as shown in the following screenshot:

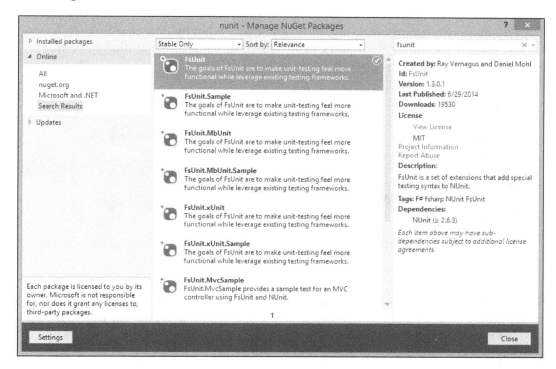

The default testing framework for FsUnit is NUnit. If you want to use another testing framework, you need to find the **FsUnit** package for that framework. There are both FsUnit.xUnit and Fs30Unit.MsTest.

The first time you run this test, you will most probably get a `MethodNotFoundException` exception, which will look like this:

```
Test Name: midsummer eve in 2014 should occur Jun 19

Test FullName: chapter03.nunit._1232OS_03_07.midsummer eve in 2014
should occur Jun 19

Test Source: D:\code\nunit\1232OS_03_07.fs : line 27

Test Outcome: Failed

Test Duration: 0:00:00.001


Result Message: System.MissingMethodException : Method not found:
'Void FsUnit.TopLevelOperators.should(Microsoft.FSharp.Core.
FSharpFunc`2<!!0,!!1>, !!0, System.Object)'.
```

```
Result StackTrace: at chapter05.nunit._1232OS_03_07.midsummer eve in
2014 should occur Jun 19()
```

The reason for this is that FsUnit was not compiled with the same version of Fsharp. Core that you're currently running. This can be amended by downloading the source for FsUnit and compiling it, or you can add the following configuration to your App.config file in the test project:

```xml
<?xml version="1.0" encoding="utf-8"?>
<configuration>
  <runtime>
    <assemblyBinding xmlns="urn:schemas-microsoft-com:asm.v1">
      <dependentAssembly>
        <assemblyIdentity name="FSharp.Core" publicKeyToken="b03f5f7f1
1d50a3a" culture="neutral" />
        <bindingRedirect oldVersion="0.0.0.0-4.3.1.0"
newVersion="4.3.1.0"/>
      </dependentAssembly>
    </assemblyBinding>
  </runtime>
</configuration>
```

This will tell the test runner, when looking for an assembly version of FSharp.Core lesser than 4.3.1.0, to use 4.3.1.0 instead. Exchange the version number here with the current version of F# that you're running.

You are now ready to start writing tests with FsUnit.

ReSharper test runner

There is a Visual Studio extension called ReSharper, produced by JetBrains, that contains a lot of goodies to increase productivity within Visual Studio. This product comes with a license fee, which is reasonable for the production gains you will experience while writing C# code, but as for F#, the tool has no real application at all.

I'm mentioning it here because most F# developers come from a C# developer background and have heard of this tool or owned it in the past.

What you gain from this tool, in the context of this book, is a much better test runner than the one built into Visual Studio, for the following reasons:

- It provides a hierarchical view of test cases
- You can filter tests on their statuses
- You can create different test sessions

- You can see the complete output of the test
- You can export test results in different formats
- It executes faster than Visual Studio Test Explorer

All in all, it is a better test runner that will help you succeed when your test suite expands from a few hundred tests to a couple of thousands and you need to start organizing them:

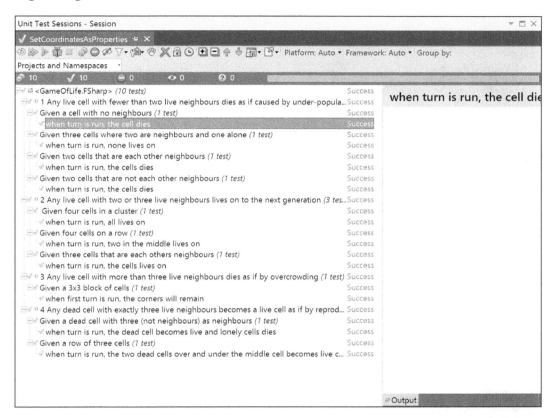

In this example, I showed how a hierarchical test suite will look when writing tests for the GameOfLife project. The GameOfLife project itself has four distinct rules we use for the basis of the hierarchy, and from there, we break the problem into smaller parts.

This gives our tests the context and provides the needed structure when you have a large quantity of tests for your system.

xUnit.net

If you try to run xUnit.net tests from ReSharper, Visual Studio will tell you it can't find any in the project. ReSharper will need a plugin in order to recognize the XUnit.net `FactAttribute` attribute, as explained in the following steps:

1. Go to **ReSharper | Extension Manager** in the top menu navigation.

2. Search for **xUnit** and find the **xUnit.net Test Support** extension. Install it, and it will enable you to execute xUnit tests within your projects, as shown in the following screenshot:

3. Restart Visual Studio and the test runner should find and execute your tests when you right-click on a project and choose **Run Tests**.

Executing a test suite outside Visual Studio

After you've succeeded in running your test suite in the development environment inside Visual Studio, it becomes increasingly important to know how to execute the test suite outside Visual Studio. In the target environment, where this code will end up, you probably won't have Visual Studio installed and sometimes may need to run the test suite to diagnose errors. So, this becomes important, especially in terms of continuous integration and having a team working on the same code base.

MSTest

In order to run MSTest tests outside of Visual Studio, you need to open the Developer Command Prompt, which comes with every version of Visual Studio. For Visual Studio 2013, they've made it a bit harder to find by hiding it in a folder called `Visual Studio Tools`, as explained in the following steps:

1. Press the Windows key to open the start menu.
2. Type `Visual Studio Tools` and click on the corresponding folder.
3. Start the Developer Command Prompt for VS2013.

If you navigate to your source code folder, you will now be able to execute the MSTest executable on your test suite:

```
>mstest /testcontainer:mstest/bin/Debug/chapter03.mstest.dll
Microsoft (R) Test Execution Command Line Tool Version 12.0.21005.1
Copyright (c) Microsoft Corporation. All rights reserved.


Loading mstest/bin/Debug/chapter03.mstest.dll...
Starting execution...


Results              Top Level Tests
-------              ---------------
Passed               mstest._12320S_03_04+CalculatorShould.add 1 and 2
with result of 3
1/1 test(s) Passed


Summary
-------
Test Run Completed.
```

```
Passed   1
---------
Total    1
Results file:  D:\code\TestResults\mikaellundin_MIKAELLUNDI35B5.trx
Test Settings: Default Test Settings
```

If you want to execute your test suite on a computer without Visual Studio, you have the possibility to just install a test agent on the machine. This is a little more lightweight than installing the whole Visual Studio development environment; it contains the MSTest executable with all its dependencies.

It is, however, not possible to execute the MSTest suite without installing any additional software.

NUnit

The NUnit test runner can be downloaded from nunit.org and installed on the machine where you want to run the tests, but personally, I prefer including the test runner as a NuGet package to the solution instead:

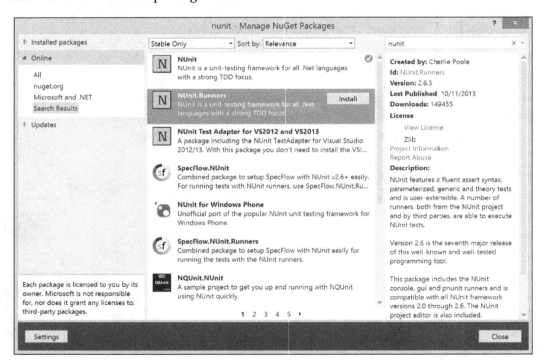

This will install everything you need in the solution directory path, `\packages\`
`NUnit.Runners.2.6.3\tools`.

In order to execute the tests from a graphical user interface, open up `nunit.exe` and
add the test assembly to it:

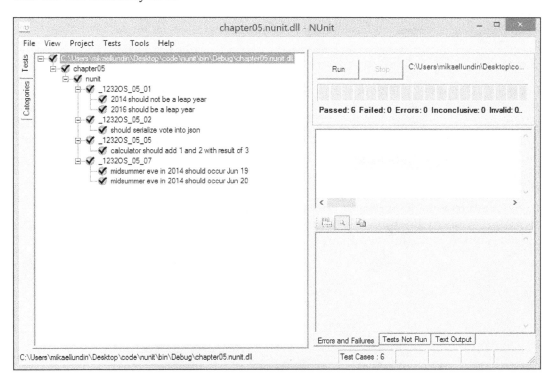

You can also execute the test suite from the Command Prompt:

```
>packages\NUnit.Runners.2.6.3\tools\nunit-console.exe nunit\bin\Debug\
chapter03.nunit.dll
```

```
NUnit-Console version 2.6.3.13283
```

```
Copyright (C) 2002-2012 Charlie Poole.
```

```
Copyright (C) 2002-2004 James W. Newkirk, Michael C. Two, Alexei A.
Vorontsov.
```

```
Copyright (C) 2000-2002 Philip Craig.
```

```
All Rights Reserved.
```

```
Runtime Environment -
   OS Version: Microsoft Windows NT 6.2.9200.0
```

```
CLR Version: 2.0.50727.8009 ( Net 3.5 )


ProcessModel: Default    DomainUsage: Single
Execution Runtime: net-3.5

......

Tests run: 6, Errors: 0, Failures: 0, Inconclusive: 0, Time:
0.5967672495353 seconds
  Not run: 0, Invalid: 0, Ignored: 0, Skipped: 0
```

Because NUnit doesn't have any external dependencies, it is suitable to just copy NUnit.Runner to the machine where and when tests are needed. As for build servers, you can commit the test runner to a source control, as you have the same version of the test runner running on a test suite and using the same version of the NUnit framework.

xUnit

If you want to execute the xUnit test suite outside Visual Studio, you need to use NuGet in order to download the **xUnit.net: Runners** package from the official NuGet feed, as shown in the following screenshot:

This will install the binaries at `packages/xunit.runners.1.9.2/tools`, based on your solution directory.

If you open up the XUnit.net test runner GUI, you can easily add the binary and run your tests. This is useful to quickly determine whether a test suite is green on a different computer than the developer machine:

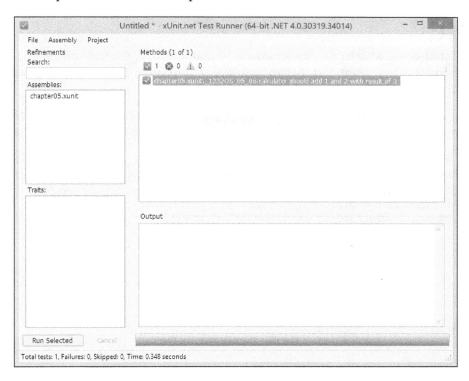

We can also easily execute the tests from the Command Prompt, giving us some easy integration with build servers and other continuous integration tools, as follows:

```
>packages\xunit.runners.1.9.2\tools\xunit.console.clr4.exe xunit\bin\
Debug\chapter03.xunit.dll
```

```
xUnit.net console test runner (64-bit .NET 4.0.30319.34014)
Copyright (C) 2013 Outercurve Foundation.


xunit.dll:     Version 1.9.2.1705
Test assembly: D:\code\xunit\bin\Debug\chapter03.xunit.dll


1 total, 0 failed, 0 skipped, took 0.334 seconds
```

This concludes the section on how to execute your test suite outside of Visual Studio. As we've already seen, the support for this is quite weak for MSTest, but stronger for both NUnit and xUnit. This might be important in terms of the portability of your code when you want to execute the test suite on more machines than just the developer machines and affect the choice of your framework.

FAKE

The point of being able to run tests outside Visual Studio is not something you will have to do very often, but it is an absolute requirement to run your tests in a build script.

FAKE is a build automation system similar to the make of C and the rake of Ruby, featuring F# with a specific **Domain Specific Language (DSL)** to set up build scripts fast and easy.

To get started, install the NuGet package for FAKE in your solution. You don't have to add it to any particular project. This is shown in the following screenshot:

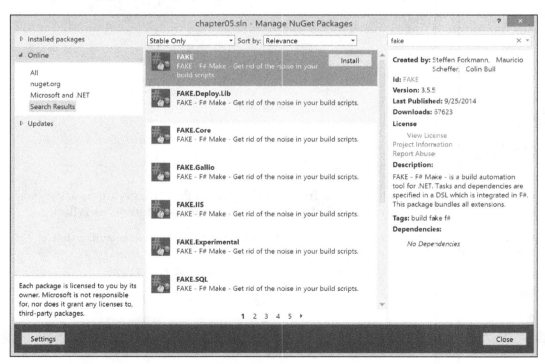

The package will install itself on the solution directory path, `packages\FAKE.3.5.5\` `tools`. Now, in the solution level, create a new F# script file called `build.fsx`:

```
// define includes
#I @"packages/FAKE.3.5.5/tools/"
#r @"FakeLib.dll"
open Fake
open Fake.FileUtils

// constants
let buildDir = "./build"
let deployDir = "./deploy"

// define targets
Target "Clean" (fun _ ->
    CleanDirs [buildDir; deployDir]
)

// define dependencies

// execute
Run "Clean"
```

The only thing this build script does is remove the build directory if it exists and adds a new one. It is a shell of the beginning of a FAKE build script. When we run it, the output looks like this:

```
>fsi build.fsx
Building project with version: LocalBuild
Shortened DependencyGraph for Target Clean:
<== Clean

The resulting target order is:
 - Clean
Starting Target: Clean
Deleting contents of ./build
Creating D:\code\deploy
Finished Target: Clean

----------------------------------------------------------------
```

```
Build Time Report
-------------------------------------------------------------------
Target      Duration
------      --------
Clean       00:00:00.0114626
Total:      00:00:00.0417724
Status:     Ok
-------------------------------------------------------------------
```

This is very verbose and clearly shows that a build directory is removed and then created. Let's add some compiling to the mix:

```
Target "BuildTest" (fun _ ->
    let projectFiles = !! (srcDir + "/**/*.fsproj")
    MSBuildDebug testDir "Build" projectFiles
        |> Log "Test build: "
)
```

This piece of code will debug and build the project files and output the result to the test directory. Now all we need to do is execute these tests in the output directory, as follows:

```
Target "Test" (fun _ ->
    // mstest
    [testDir + "/chapter03.mstest.dll"]
      |> MSTest (fun p -> p)

    // nunit
    [testDir + "/chapter03.nunit.dll"]
      |> NUnit (fun p ->
        { p with
            DisableShadowCopy = true;
            ToolPath = "./packages/NUnit.Runners.2.6.3/tools";
            OutputFile = testDir + "/chapter03.nunit-TestResults.xml"}
      )

    // xunit
    [testDir + "/chapter03.xunit.dll"]
      |> xUnit (fun p ->
        { p with
            ToolPath = "./packages/xunit.runners.1.9.2/tools/xunit.
console.clr4.exe";
            ShadowCopy = false;
            HtmlOutput = true;
```

```
                    XmlOutput = true;
                    OutputDir = testDir
            }
        )
    )
```

This target now runs all our test suites: MSTest, NUnit, and xUnit. It does so by using the command-line tools we tried out in the previous chapter. Sometimes, FAKE will be able to figure out where this tool is, for example, MSTest, where the binary exists in the system path. As for NUnit and xUnit, we merely point out the `ToolPath` path where we installed the NuGet packages for these runners.

After running the test suite, we get this report:

```
-------------------------------------------------------------------

Build Time Report

-------------------------------------------------------------------

Target      Duration

------      --------

Clean       00:00:00.0194436

BuildTest   00:00:00.8076760

Test        00:00:04.0909364

Total:      00:00:04.9540847

Status:     Ok

-------------------------------------------------------------------
```

We can now continue to expand this script by building the release version of the code, creating deployment packages, and sending them off to a continuous deployment server. The possibilities are endless, and the best thing is that your version will control the build script together with the rest of the code.

Continuous integration

Two of the largest risks of having tests is that they will not be run or even pass. This is what will happen if you have a test suite without experienced developers maintaining it. In this case, it will no longer bring value, but only baggage. A test suite that is not used and doesn't pass is a waste and should either be fixed or deleted.

I was once working on quite an advanced order flow. To maintain its quality by myself, I covered the solution with tests knowing that if my tests were green, the code would work as expected.

I handed over the code to a maintenance team and after six months, they called me up asking me to fix the code. They were going to make some changes, and when they did, the price calculation no longer matched up. "So, are the tests passing?" I asked them. It turned out the developers had inactivated the test suite when the first test turned red.

It is easy to avoid this by having continuous integration run the tests every time code is committed to source control, and send "you broke the build" e-mails when the tests fail. For some reason, there is a psychological barrier between the developer and the build server, making it a farther step to actually inactivate the tests in the build server.

If you inactivate the tests, you do it on your machine. If you break the build, you break it for the whole team.

Git Hooks

I'm a big fan of **Git**. My first large aha! moment was finding out I could perform version control without affecting anyone else on the team, as I could commit only to my local machine.

Git led me to commit code much more often and split tasks into units of work, where each unit could be committed with a single purpose message. This results in a very nice and readable version history.

The third was about finding out that I could branch everything, which led me to have the kind of flexibility in my workstream I never had before. Whenever a client rushed in to have a critical issue fixed right away, I didn't have to stash away the things I was currently working on, risking to mix them up with the fix. Instead, I just created a new fix branch from the master.

I'm not going to go into the details of how I use Git, but there is one aspect of it that I really like, concerning test automation.

This is the workflow when you work with a centralized repository:

1. Finish your code.
2. Execute your tests.
3. Commit the code to the **Version Control System** (VCS).
4. Continuous integration runs.
5. Report from the **Continuous Integration** (CI) build.

Every so often, developers, myself included, forget to perform step 2 before committing code to source control, leading to a failed build report from the continuous integration.

This would be no problem, except that the code is now committed to the central location, meaning it would affect the whole team. If the fix is particularly hard, it might hinder other developers to commit their code for several hours while you fix your failed build.

Even worse, other developers might not notice the failed build and commit code on top of the already failing build, making matters worse.

Git Hooks comes to the rescue!

Git lets us define scripts that should run before certain actions occur. These actions can be grouped into the server side and client side. Client-side hooks are those that will solve the problems I just stated.

Let's create a precommit hook that will run our tests before we commit code. Add the following line of code to the `.git/hooks/pre-commit` file:

```
#!/bin/sh
fsi build.fsx Test
```

By using the build script we created in the previous section, we will now execute the tests before committing the code. The build script will return a nonzero result if the test fails, causing Git to abort the commit. However, if the build is successful and returns 0, Git will go ahead and commit the changes.

This means we'll not be able to commit any changes to the **Distributed Version Control System (DVCS)** without making the tests pass. If the build fails in the build server, it will no longer be because we failed to run our tests locally.

In the same spirit, you can use a prepush hook to query the continuous integration server that the build has not failed before it is allowed to push more code. This way, we can avoid pushing more code to an already failing build.

TeamCity

TeamCity is one of the most prominent build servers for the .NET platform. It has taken over the continuous integration market, which you will understand unless you've completely invested in **Team Foundation Server (TFS)** and are forced to use TF Build.

TeamCity can be downloaded and installed from **JetBrains** and is free to use for open source projects. It will install itself as one of few Windows services that represent the build server controller and the agents that run the build.

We're now going to dive into how to set up a new build and run your tests through TeamCity.

1. Start by creating a new project, as shown in the following screenshot:

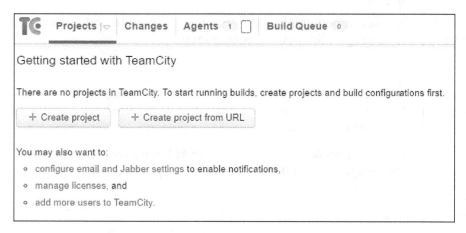

2. Enter the basic information about your project:

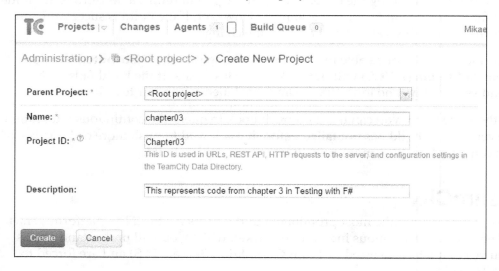

3. The next step is to create a build configuration. Normally, you have a compile step and then a test step, but for brevity, we'll skip immediately to the test step:

4. For code repository, I'm using Git and GitHub for this example. I will now enter the following details into the TeamCity VCS configuration:

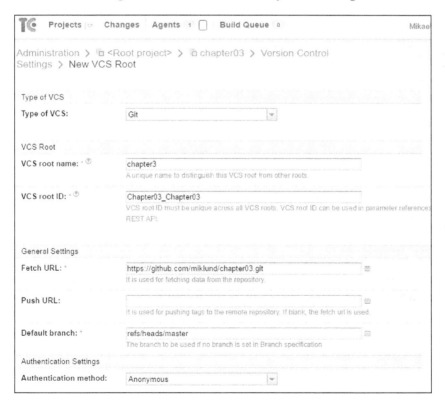

5. Next up, it's time to configure the build steps. First, we need to restore the NuGet packages from the NuGet Package Feed because we're not committing the packages to source control, as shown in the following screenshot:

6. Next comes the command-line build step that will execute the FAKE build script, which will run the tests, as shown in the following screenshot:

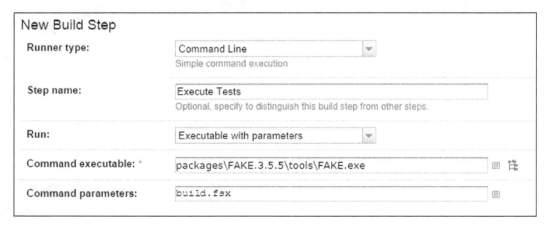

7. Before running the build, we need to define some artifacts where the test results will be stored, as shown in the following screenshot:

Name: *	Test	
Build configuration ID: * ⓘ	Chapter03_Test	Regenerate ID
	This ID is used in URLs, REST API, HTTP requests to the server, and configuration settings in the TeamCity Data Directory.	
Description:	Run the tests for the code	

Artifact paths: ⓘ	`/output/test/mstest.XML`
	`/output/test/chapter03.xunit.dll.xml`
	`/output/test/chapter03.nunit-TestResults.xml`
		🗑 📁

	Newline-separated paths of files or directories to publish as build artifacts. Ant-style wildcards like `dir/**/*.zip` and target directories like `out/*.zip => dist`, where `dist` is a target directory are supported. The paths can also be separated by commas.	

8. Now, we can run the build. It will download all the required packages from the NuGet feed and then continue running our tests from the FAKE build script, as shown in the following screenshot:

The only thing left to do is set up a trigger so the build will run automatically every time a developer commits code, and then you'll be able to set up with continuous integration together with the F# project and tests.

Summary

In this chapter, we looked at how to get started and set up your environment for unit testing. We learned about three testing frameworks, along with their strengths and weaknesses, and saw that we can, without breaking a sweat, get started with all three in F#.

We also learned how to take testing with F# a step further, outside of Visual Studio and into our development process and continuous integration.

In the next chapter, we will dive deep into unit testing, all the techniques for writing good unit tests, and how to apply these with F#.

4
Unit Testing

Unit testing is the art of designing your program in such a way that you can easily test each function as isolated units and such verify its correctness. Unit testing is not only a tool for verification of functionality, but also mostly a tool for designing that functionality in a testable way. What you gain is the means of finding problems early, facilitating change, documentation, and design.

In this chapter, we will dive into how to write good unit tests using F#:

- Structuring your tests
- Testing in isolation
- Finding the abstraction level
- Test doubles
- Dependency injection
- Dealing with databases

After reading this chapter, you will be able to write high-quality unit tests that will require little maintenance and stand the test of refactoring, interface changes, and maintenance.

Structuring your tests

The most basic aspect of unit testing is figuring out how to structure your tests. The most common way to structure when writing tests after code is to mimic the namespace hierarchy for your system under a test in another Visual Studio project.

We write our class as follows:

```
namespace Company.System.BL.Calculators
{
    public class PriceCalculator
```

```
    {
        public double GetPrice(object order)
        {
            return .0;
        }
    }
}
```

Then, our test would look like the following:

```
namespace Company.System.Tests.BL.Calculators
{
    public class PriceCalculatorTests
    {
        [Test]
        public void GetPriceShould()
        {
            // ...
        }
    }
}
```

Notice the differences in namespaces and naming conventions. This is a very common way to structure tests because it scales up to very large projects and is pretty straightforward.

It is clear that code is written before the tests, as the test names and hierarchy are directly proportional to the code it was written for. If we start out writing the test first, then we must begin describing what the feature is and what we intend for it to do, as shown the following:

```
namespace ``PriceCalculator will calculate the price of an order``

module ``for an empty order`` =

    open Company.System.BL.Calculators

    open NUnit.Framework

    let priceCalculator = PriceCalculator()

    type Order = { OrderLines : string list}
    let order = { OrderLines = []}
```

```
[<Test>]
let ``the price should be 0`` () =
    let result = priceCalculator.GetPrice(order)
    Assert.That(result, Is.EqualTo(0))
```

This code is a bit messy, and we will address that shortly, but first let's look at what it really does, line by line:

- **#1**: The namespace declaration is the root level of the test tree and represents the user story that is being worked on

- **#3**: The module declaration is the scenario for the user story

- **#15**: The test function is the assertion

The reason for writing tests like this becomes obvious when looking at the test output. It describes the system and what it is supposed to do, and not just what we expect of the code that has already been written, as shown in the following screenshot:

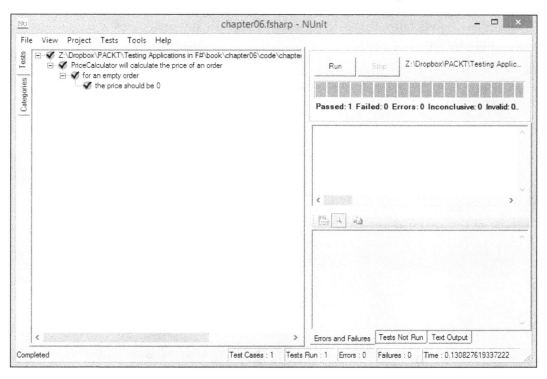

The beauty here is, of course, that you can read out the functionality of the test structure and hierarchy. The main difference between this and the old way of writing tests is that here, you document what the function is supposed to do, and previously, we only verified that the written code did what it was supposed to. This new way of writing tests, is ultimately driving the function and design of the code.

Arrange, act, assert

To bring order into our unit tests, there are certain patterns to follow. One of the most common and popular patterns is the triple A (AAA) syntax, where the A's stand for:

- Arrange
- Act
- Assert

The best way to visualize this is in code. Let's see how it works in C# code and then move on to the F# equivalent:

```
using NUnit.Framework;
using SUT = Company.System.BL.Calculators;

namespace Company.System.Tests.BL.Calculators.PriceCalculator
{
    public class GetPrice
    {
        [Test]
        public void ShouldReturnZeroOnEmptyOrder()
        {
            // Arrange
            var priceCalculator = new SUT.PriceCalculator();
            var order = new { };

            // Act
            var result = priceCalculator.GetPrice(order)

            // Assert
            Assert.That(result, Is.EqualTo(0), "Expecting zero price
when order is empty");
        }
    }
}
```

I usually put the comments in there, to communicate to the reader that I'm using the AAA syntax, but also to make my intentions clear of where the line is drawn between arrange, act, and assert.

In the **arrange** segment of this code, we instantiate all the dependencies our test has, and we also set up all the state that is necessary for the test to go through. If we need to set up mocks or stubs, we do this in the arrange section.

The arrange section is simply everything we need to run the test. The **act** section is the reason the test exists, and should only consist of one line of code. This line of code should call into the **System Under Test (SUT)** in order to test what we want to verify. This act statement usually assigns the result to a result variable, but not necessarily so, as the SUT could have updated some mutated state that we'll verify. The assert section verifies that the result of running the test was successful.

Sometimes, you need some helping code to extract the result, but mostly the assert section is also only one line of code. It is crucial for the test design to assert only one thing in each test.

Now, what happens when we apply this to our F# sample?

```
[<Test>]
let ''the price should be 0'' () =
    // arrange
    let priceCalculator = PriceCalculator()
    let order = { OrderLines = []}

    // act
    let result = priceCalculator.GetPrice(order)

    // assert
    Assert.That(result, Is.EqualTo(0))
```

It actually works very well. We will come back to this later when touching upon the framework FsUnit and how the AAA syntax applies there. It is also of great interest when doing mocking, as it provides a greater structure when writing unit tests.

Separate project versus inline tests

A hardware engineer hearing about unit testing in software for the first time might be found saying, we've been doing that for years. It is called a self-test when a hardware circuit is able to perform testing of its functions by sending itself the correct signal.

This means some of our hardware is shipping with tests. So, why are we going to such lengths in software to ship without tests?

```
// get the items from l1 that are not in l2
let difference l1 l2 = (set l1) - (set l2) |> Set.toList

open NUnit.Framework

[<Test>]
let ``difference between [1..10] and [1; 3; 5; 7; 9] is [2; 4; 6; 8;
10]`` () =
    // arrange
    let l1 = [1..10]
    let l2 = [1; 3; 5; 7; 9]

    // act
    let result = difference l1 l2

    // assert
    Assert.That(result, Is.EqualTo([2; 4; 6; 8; 10]))

[<Test>]
let ``difference between [1..10] and [] is [1..10]`` () =
    // arrange
    let l1 = [1..10]
    let l2 = []

    // act
    let result = difference l1 l2

    // assert
    Assert.That(result, Is.EqualTo([1..10]))
```

When looking this code, it's so painstakingly obvious that after writing a function you would add some tests for that function just underneath it.

- Your test is the closest possible to what it's testing
- Your test can test and modify `private` members of the SUT
- Your tests, by definition of what the system does, is part of the system itself

Turning it around, we could write the tests before the actual implementation:

```
namespace ``difference between a and b``

module ``when a is one-to-ten and b is even numbers`` =

    open NUnit.Framework
```

```fsharp
    // arrange
    let a = [1..10]
    let b = [2; 4; 6; 8; 10]

    [<Test>]
    let ``expected result is [1; 3; 5; 7; 9]`` () =
        // act
        let result = difference a b

        // assert
        CollectionAssert.AreEqual([1; 3; 5; 7; 9], result)

module ``when a is one-to-ten and b is one-to-ten`` =

    open NUnit.Framework
    open chapter06.fsharp._1232OS_06_06

    // arrange
    let a = [1..10]
    let b = [1..10]

    [<Test>]
    let ``expected result is empty List`` () =
        // act
        let result = difference a b

        // assert
        CollectionAssert.IsEmpty(result)
```

The first thing you notice is that the tests have a very loose coupling to the actual implementation. Instead, the tests only state what the supposed functionality is supposed to do, and not what the already existing functionality does.

This is one way to create distance between the tests and the actual implementation.

- Tests describe the functionality, instead of retrofitting what the code does
- The SUT is forced to present a public interface for the test to call
- It's better at driving the design of the code

Should this piece of code be in the same project or another project? In my honest opinion, it doesn't matter. Having both SUT and code in the same project but separating them by other means would make some continuous integration tasks easier, but it would also bring unnecessary dependencies into production. It appears to be a give or take scenario.

FsUnit

The current state of unit testing in F# is good. You can get all the major test frameworks running with little effort, but there is still something that feels a bit off with the way tests and asserts are expressed:

```
open NUnit.Framework
Assert.That(result, Is.EqualTo(42))
```

Using FsUnit, you can achieve much higher expressiveness in writing unit tests by simply reversing the way the assert is written:

```
open FsUnit
result |> should equal 42
```

Please refer to *Chapter 3, Setting Up Your Test Environment*, on how to set up a testing environment with FsUnit.

The FsUnit framework is not a test runner in itself, but uses an underlying test framework to execute. The underlying framework can be of MSTest, NUnit, or xUnit. FsUnit can best be explained as having a different structure and syntax while writing tests.

While this is a more dense syntax, the need for structure still exists and AAA is more needed more than ever. Consider the following test example:

```
[<Measure>] type EUR
[<Measure>] type SEK
type Country = | Sweden | Germany | France


let calculateVat country (amount : float<'u>) =
    match country with
    | Sweden -> amount * 0.25
    | Germany -> amount * 0.19
    | France -> amount * 0.2

open NUnit.Framework
open FsUnit

[<Test>]
let ``Sweden should have 25% VAT`` () =
    let amount = 200.<SEK>

    calculateVat Sweden amount |> should equal 50<SEK>
```

This code will calculate the VAT in Sweden in Swedish currency. What is interesting is that when we break down the test code and see that it actually follows the AAA structure, even it doesn't explicitly tell us this is so:

```
[<Test>]
let ``Germany should have 19% VAT`` () =
    // arrange
    let amount = 200.<EUR>
    // act
    calculateVat Germany amount
    //assert
    |> should equal 38<EUR>
```

The only thing I did here was add the annotations for AAA. It gives us the perspective of what we're doing, what frames we're working inside, and the rules for writing good unit tests.

Assertions

We have already seen the `equal` assertion, which verifies that the test result is equal to the expected value. This is, by far, the most common assertion you will need:

```
result |> should equal 42
```

You can negate this assertion by using the `not'` statement, as follows:

```
result |> should not' (equal 43)
```

With strings, it's quite common to assert that a string starts or ends with some value, as follows:

```
"$12" |> should startWith "$"
"$12" |> should endWith "12"
```

And, you can also negate that, as follows:

```
"$12" |> should not' (startWith "€")
"$12" |> should not' (endWith "14")
```

You can verify that a result is within a boundary. This will, in turn, verify that the result is somewhere between the values of `35-45`:

```
result |> should (equalWithin 5) 40
```

And, you can also negate that, as follows:

```
result |> should not' ((equalWithin 1) 40)
```

With the collection types list, array, and sequence, you can check that it contains a specific value:

```
[1..10] |> should contain 5
```

And, you can also negate it to verify that a value is missing, as follows:

```
[1; 1; 2; 3; 5; 8; 13] |> should not' (contain 7)
```

It is common to test the boundaries of a function and then its exception handling. This means you need to be able to assert exceptions, as follows:

```
let getPersonById id = failwith "id cannot be less than 0"
(fun () -> getPersonById -1 |> ignore) |> should throw
typeof<System.Exception>
```

There is a be function that can be used in a lot of interesting ways. Even in situations where the equal assertion can replace some of these be structures, we can opt for a more semantic way of expressing our assertions, providing better error messages.

Let us see examples of this, as follows:

```
// true or false
1 = 1 |> should be True
1 = 2 |> should be False

// strings as result
"" |> should be EmptyString
null |> should be NullOrEmptyString

// null is nasty in functional programming
[] |> should not' (be Null)

// same reference
let person1 = new System.Object()
let person2 = person1
person1 |> should be (sameAs person2)

// not same reference, because copy by value
let a = System.DateTime.Now
let b = a
a |> should not' (be (sameAs b))

// greater and lesser
result |> should be (greaterThan 0)
```

```
result |> should not' (be lessThan 0)

// of type
result |> should be ofExactType<int>

// list assertions
[] |> should be Empty
[1; 2; 3] |> should not' (be Empty)
```

With this, you should be able to assert most of the things you're looking for. But there still might be a few edge cases out there that default FsUnit asserts won't catch.

Custom assertions

FsUnit is extensible, which makes it easy to add your own assertions on top of the chosen test runner. This has the possibility of making your tests extremely readable.

The first example will be a custom assert which verifies that a given string matches a regular expression. This will be implemented using NUnit as a framework, as follows:

```
open FsUnit
open NUnit.Framework.Constraints
open System.Text.RegularExpressions

// NUnit: implement a new assert
type MatchConstraint(n) =
    inherit Constraint() with
        override this.WriteDescriptionTo(writer : MessageWriter) :
unit =
            writer.WritePredicate("matches")
            writer.WriteExpectedValue(sprintf "%s" n)
        override this.Matches(actual : obj) =
            match actual with
            | :? string as input -> Regex.IsMatch(input, n)
            | _ -> failwith "input must be of string type"

let match' n = MatchConstraint(n)


open NUnit.Framework

[<Test>]
let ``NUnit custom assert`` () =
    "2014-10-11" |> should match' "\d{4}-\d{2}-\d{2}"
    "11/10 2014" |> should not' (match' "\d{4}-\d{2}-\d{2}")
```

In order to create your own assert, you need to create a type that implements the `NUnit.Framework.Constraints.IConstraint` interface, and this is easily done by inheriting from the `Constraint` base class.

You need to override both the `WriteDescriptionTo()` and `Matches()` method, where the first one controls the message that will be output from the test, and the second is the actual test. In this implementation, I verify that input is a string; or the test will fail. Then, I use the `Regex.IsMatch()` static function to verify the match.

Next, we create an alias for the `MatchConstraint()` function, `match'`, with the extra apostrophe to avoid conflict with the internal F# match expression, and then we can use it as any other `assert` function in FsUnit.

Doing the same for xUnit requires a completely different implementation. First, we need to add a reference to NHamcrest API. We'll find it by searching for the package in the **NuGet Package Manager**:

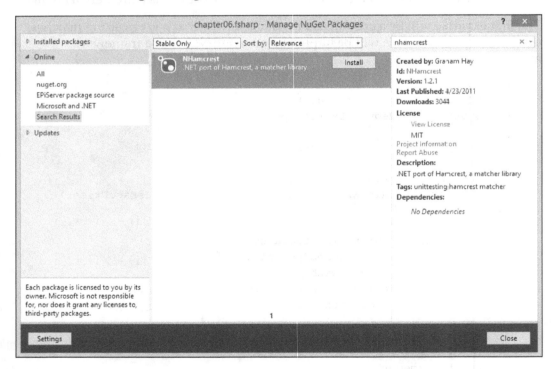

Instead, we make an implementation that uses the NHamcrest API, which is a .NET port of the Java Hamcrest library for building matchers for test expressions, shown as follows:

```
open System.Text.RegularExpressions
open NHamcrest
open NHamcrest.Core

// test assertion for regular expression matching
let match' pattern =
    CustomMatcher<obj>(sprintf "Matches %s" pattern, fun c ->
        match c with
        | :? string as input -> Regex.IsMatch(input, pattern)
        | _ -> false)

open Xunit
open FsUnit.Xunit

[<Fact>]
let ``Xunit custom assert`` () =
    "2014-10-11" |> should match' "\d{4}-\d{2}-\d{2}"
    "11/10 2014" |> should not' (match' "\d{4}-\d{2}-\d{2}")
```

The functionality in this implementation is the same as the NUnit version, but the implementation here is much easier. We create a function that receives an argument and return a `CustomMatcher<obj>` object. This will only take the output message from the test and the function to test the match.

Writing an assertion for FsUnit driven by MSTest works exactly the same way as it would in Xunit, by NHamcrest creating a `CustomMatcher<obj>` object.

Unquote

There is another F# assertion library that is completely different from FsUnit but with different design philosophies accomplishes the same thing, by making F# unit tests more functional. Just like FsUnit, this library provides the means of writing assertions, but relies on NUnit as a testing framework.

Instead of working with a DSL like FsUnit or API such as with the NUnit framework, the **Unquote** library assertions are based on F# code quotations.

Code quotations is a quite unknown feature of F# where you can turn any code into an abstract syntax tree. Namely, when the F# compiler finds a code quotation in your source file, it will not compile it, but rather expand it into a syntax tree that represents an F# expression.

The following is an example of a code quotation:

```
<@ 1 + 1 @>
```

If we execute this in F# Interactive, we'll get the following output:

```
val it : Quotations.Expr =
  Call (None, op_Addition, [Value (1), Value (1)])
```

This is truly code as data, and we can use it to write code that operates on code as if it was data, which in this case, it is. It brings us closer to what a compiler does, and gives us lots of power in the metadata programming space.

We can use this to write assertions with Unquote. Start by including the **Unquote** NuGet package in your test project, as shown in the following screenshot:

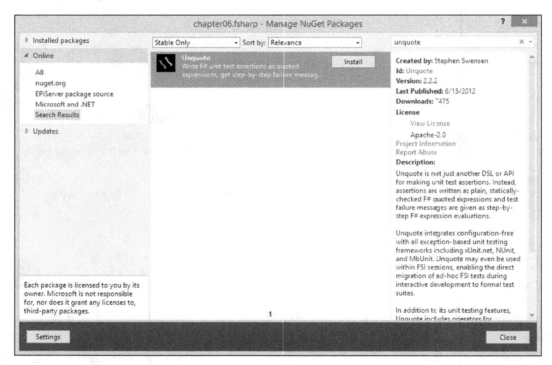

And now, we can implement our first test using Unquote, as follows:

```
open NUnit.Framework
open Swensen.Unquote

[<Test>]
let ``Fibonacci sequence should start with 1, 1, 2, 3, 5`` () =
    test <@ fibonacci |> Seq.take 5 |> List.ofSeq = [1; 1; 2; 3; 5] @>
```

This works by Unquote first finding the equals operation, and then reducing each side of the equals sign until they are equal or no longer able to reduce.

Writing a test that fails and watching the output more easily explains this. The following test should fail because 9 is not a prime number:

```
[<Test>]
let ``prime numbers under 10 are 2, 3, 5, 7, 9`` () =
    test <@ primes 10 = [2; 3; 5; 7; 9] @> // fail
```

The test will fail with the following message:

```
Test Name:  prime numbers under 10 are 2, 3, 5, 7, 9

Test FullName:  chapter04.prime numbers under 10 are 2, 3, 5, 7, 9

Test Outcome:  Failed

Test Duration:  0:00:00.077


Result Message:
primes 10 = [2; 3; 5; 7; 9]
[2; 3; 5; 7] = [2; 3; 5; 7; 9]
false


Result StackTrace:
at Microsoft.FSharp.Core.Operators.Raise[T](Exception exn)
at chapter04.prime numbers under 10 are 2, 3, 5, 7, 9()
```

In the resulting message, we can see both sides of the equals sign reduced until only `false` remains. It's a very elegant way of breaking down a complex assertion.

Assertions

The assertions in Unquote are not as specific or extensive as the ones in FsUnit. The idea of having lots of specific assertions for different situations is to get very descriptive error messages when the tests fail. Since Unquote actually outputs the whole reduction of the statements when the test fails, the need for explicit assertions is not that high. You'll get a descript error message anyway. The absolute most common is to check for equality, as shown before. You can also verify that two expressions are not equal:

```
test <@ 1 + 2 = 4 - 1 @>
test <@ 1 + 2 <> 4 @>
```

We can check whether a value is greater or smaller than the expected value:

```
test <@ 42 < 1337 @>
test <@ 1337 > 42 @>
```

You can check for a specific exception, or just any exception:

```
raises<System.NullReferenceException> <@ (null : string).Length @>
raises<exn> <@ System.String.Format(null, null) @>
```

Here, the `Unquote` syntax excels compared to FsUnit, which uses a unit lambda expression to do the same thing in a quirky way.

The Unquote library also has its reduce functionality in the public AFI, making it possible for you to reduce and analyze an expression. Using the `reduceFully` syntax, we can get the reduction in a list, as shown in the following:

```
> <@ (1+2)/3 @> |> reduceFully |> List.map decompile;;
val it : string list = ["(1 + 2) / 3"; "3 / 3"; "1"]
```

If we just want the output to console output, we can run the `unquote` command directly:

```
> unquote <@ [for i in 1..5 -> i * i] = ([1..5] |> List.map (fun i -> i *
i)) @>;;
Seq.toList (seq (Seq.delay (fun () -> Seq.map (fun i -> i * i) {1..5})))
= ([1..5] |> List.map (fun i -> i * i))
Seq.toList (seq seq [1; 4; 9; 16; ...]) = ([1; 2; 3; 4; 5] |> List.map
(fun i -> i * i))
Seq.toList seq [1; 4; 9; 16; ...] = [1; 4; 9; 16; 25]
[1; 4; 9; 16; 25] = [1; 4; 9; 16; 25]
true
```

It is important to know what tools are out there, and Unquote is one of those tools that is fantastic to know about when you run into a testing problem in which you want to reduce both sides of an equals sign. Most often, this belongs to difference computations or algorithms like price calculation.

We have also seen that Unquote provides a great way of expressing tests for exceptions that is unmatched by FsUnit.

Testing in isolation

One of the most important aspects of unit testing is to test in isolation. This does not only mean to fake any external dependency, but also that the test code itself should not be tied up to some other test code.

If you're not testing in isolation, there is a potential risk that your test fails. This is not because of the system under test, but the state that has lingered from a previous test run, or external dependencies.

Writing pure functions without any state is one way of making sure your test runs in isolation. Another way is by making sure that the test creates all the needed state itself.

- Shared state, like connections, between tests is a bad idea
- Using TestFixtureSetUp/TearDown attributes to set up a state for a set of tests is a bad idea
- Keeping low performance resources around because they're expensive to set up is a bad idea

The most common shared states are the following:

- The ASP.NET **Model View Controller (MVC)** session state
- Dependency injection setup
- Database connection, even though it is no longer strictly a unit test

Here's how one should think about unit testing in isolation, as shown in the following screenshot:

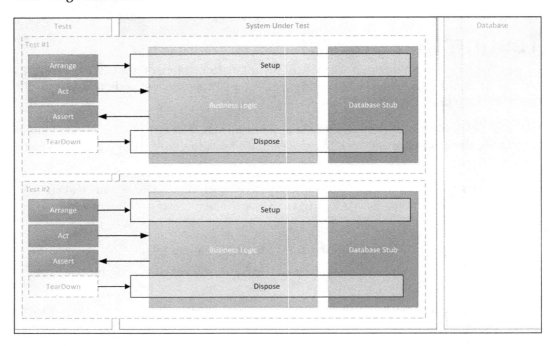

Each test is responsible for setting up the SUT and its database/web service stubs in order to perform the test and assert on the result. It is equally important that the test cleans up after itself, which in the case of unit tests most often can be handed over to the garbage collector, and doesn't need to be explicitly disposed. It is common to think that one should only isolate a test fixture from other test fixtures, but this idea of a test fixture is bad. Instead, one should strive for having each test stand for itself to as large an extent as possible, and not be dependent on outside setups. This does not mean you will have unnecessary long unit tests, provided you write SUT and tests well within that context.

The problem we often run into is that the SUT itself maintains some kind of state that is present between tests. The state can simply be a value that is set in the application domain and is present between different test runs, as follows:

```
let getCustomerFullNameByID id =
    if cache.ContainsKey(id) then
        (cache.[id] :?> Customer).FullName
    else
        // get from database
        // NOTE: stub code
```

```
let customer = db.getCustomerByID id
cache.[id] <- customer
customer.FullName
```

The problem we see here is that the cache will be present from one test to another, so when the second test is running, it needs to make sure that its running with a clean cache, or the result might not be as expected.

One way to test it properly would be to separate the core logic from the cache and test them each independently. Another would be to treat it as a black box and ignore the cache completely. If the cache makes the test fail, then the functionality fails as a whole.

This depends on if we see the cache as an implementation detail of the function or a functionality by itself. Testing implementation details, or `private` functions, is dirty because our tests might break even if the functionality hasn't changed. And yet, there might be benefits into taking the implementation detail into account. In this case, we could use the cache functionality to easily stub out the database without the need of any mocking framework.

Vertical slice testing

Most often, we deal with dependencies as something we need to mock away, where as the better option would be to implement a test harness directly into the product. We know what kind of data and what kind of calls we need to make to the database, so right there, we have a public API for the database. This is often called a data access layer in a three-tier architecture (but no one ever does those anymore, right?).

As we have a public data access layer, we could easily implement an in-memory representation that can be used not only by our tests, but in development of the product, as shown in the following image:

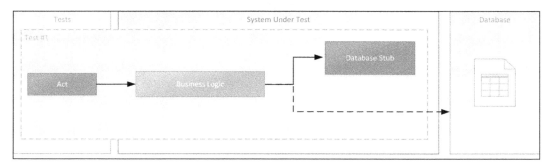

When you're running the application in development mode, you configure it toward the in-memory version of the dependency. This provides you with the following benefits:

- You'll get a faster development environment
- Your tests will become simpler
- You have complete control of your dependency

As your development environment is doing everything in memory, it becomes blazing fast. And as you develop your application, you will appreciate adjusting that public API and getting to understand completely what you expect from that dependency. It will lead to a cleaner API, where very few side effects are allowed to seep through.

Your tests will become much simpler, as instead of mocking away the dependency, you can call the in-memory dependency and set whatever state you want.

Here's an example of what a public data access API might look like:

```
type IDataAccess =
    abstract member GetCustomerByID : int -> Customer
    abstract member FindCustomerByName : string -> Customer option
    abstract member UpdateCustomerName : int -> string -> Customer
    abstract member DeleteCustomerByID : int -> bool
```

This is surely a very simple API, but it will demonstrate the point. There is a database with a customer inside it, and we want to do some operations on that.

In this case, our in-memory implementation would look like this:

```
type InMemoryDataAccess() =
    let data = new System.Collections.Generic.Dictionary<int,
Customer>()

    // expose the add method
    member this.Add customer = data.Add(customer.ID, customer)

    interface IDataAccess with
        // throw exception if not found
        member this.GetCustomerByID id =
            data.[id]

        member this.FindCustomerByName fullName =
            data.Values |> Seq.tryFind (fun customer -> customer.
FullName = fullName)
```

```
    member this.UpdateCustomerName id fullName =
        data.[id] <- { data.[id] with FullName = fullName }
        data.[id]

    member this.DeleteCustomerByID id =
        data.Remove(id)
```

This is a simple implementation that provides the same functionality as the database would, but in memory. This makes it possible to run the tests completely in isolation without worrying about mocking away the dependencies. The dependencies are already substituted with in-memory replacements, and as seen with this example, the in-memory replacement doesn't have to be very extensive.

The only extra function except from the interface implementation is the Add() function which lets us set the state prior to the test, as this is something the interface itself doesn't provide for us.

Now, in order to sew it together with the real implementation, we need to create a configuration in order to select what version to use, as shown in the following code:

```
open System.Configuration
open System.Collections.Specialized

// TryGetValue extension method to NameValueCollection
type NameValueCollection with
    member this.TryGetValue (key : string) =
        if this.Get(key) = null then
            None
        else
            Some (this.Get key)

let dataAccess : IDataAccess =
    match ConfigurationManager.AppSettings.TryGetValue("DataAccess")
with
    | Some "InMemory" -> new InMemoryDataAccess() :> IDataAccess
    | Some _ | None -> new DefaultDataAccess() :> IDataAccess

// usage
let fullName = (dataAccess.GetCustomerByID 1).FullName
```

Again, with only a few lines of code, we manage to select the appropriate IDataAccess instance and execute against it without using dependency injection or taking a penalty in code readability, as we would in C#.

The code is straightforward and easy to read, and we can execute any tests we want without touching the external dependency, or in this case, the database.

Finding the abstraction level

In order to start unit testing, you have to start writing tests; this is what they'll tell you. If you want to get good at it, just start writing tests, any and a lot of them. The rest will solve itself.

I've watched experienced developers sit around staring dumbfounded at an empty screen because they couldn't get into their mind how to get started, what to test.

The question is not unfounded. In fact, it is still debated in the **Test Driven Development (TDD)** community what should be tested. The ground rule is that the test should bring at least as much value as the cost of writing it, but that is a bad rule for someone new to testing, as all tests are expensive for them to write.

Public interface

Once your tests suite grows into a couple thousand tests, they will start breaking, not only when you change functionality and expect them to break, but when you add functionality or optimize the inner workings of a function.

This is what we call brittle tests. They break, even when the condition they're testing hasn't changed.

The reason for this is always because the test knows too much about the system that it's testing. It makes assumptions on what the implementation of the SUT looks like, and when those assumptions no longer are true, the test breaks.

To look at a brittle test scenario, we will use this string concatenation function as our SUT, as shown in the following code:

```
// implementation detail
let sb = System.Text.StringBuilder()

// concat values of a list
// BAD CODE don't do this
let concat (separator : string) (items : string list) =
    // clear from any previous concatenations
    sb.Clear()

    // append all values to string builder
    for item in items do
        sb.Append(item) |> ignore
        sb.Append(separator)

    // remove last separator
```

```
        if not items.IsEmpty then
            sb.Remove(sb.Length - separator.Length, separator.Length) |>
    ignore

        sb.ToString()
```

We all know that a `StringBuilder` class is the most efficient way of concatenating strings, but they come with a penalty of instantiation. So, we create a global `StringBuilder` class that is instantiated once, and then reuse it between concatenations. This is a good example of bad pre-optimization.

Let's look at some tests for this:

```
    [<Test>]
    let ``should remove last separator from result`` () =
        let data = ["The"; "quick"; "brown"; "fox"; "jumps"; "over";
    "the"; "lazy"; "dog"]
        concat " " data |> should not' (endWith " ")

    [<Test>]
    let ``should clear the string builder before second concatenation`` ()
    =
        let data = ["The"; "quick"; "brown"; "fox"; "jumps"; "over";
    "the"; "lazy"; "dog"]
        concat " " data |> ignore
        concat " " data |> ignore
        sb.ToString() |> should equal "The quick brown fox jumps over
    the lazy dog"
```

Both these tests state something that is true about the SUT, but they are both bad. The first test assumes that the result is built up by adding the item and separator consecutive until the end, and then the last separator is deleted. This is an implementation detail of the function.

The second test goes into even more detail about the implementation and states how the `StringBuilder` class should be used in the concatenation. These tests are both operating on a bad abstraction level.

Now, what happens when running this code in production is that it crashes unexpectedly at heavy load. It turns out, by the following test, that it is not thread-safe:

```
> let data = ['a'..'z'] |> List.map (fun c -> c.ToString())
Array.Parallel.init 51 (fun _ -> concat "" data);;
```

```
System.AggregateException: One or more errors occurred. ---> System.
ArgumentOutOfRangeException: Index was out of range. Must be non-negative
and less than the size of the collection.
Parameter name: chunkLength
    at System.Text.StringBuilder.ToString()
```

The use of the `StringBuilder` class is no longer justified and instead the SUT is rewritten to the following:

```
// no longer in use
let sb = System.Text.StringBuilder()

// concat values of a list
let concat separator = List.reduce (fun s1 s2 -> sprintf "%s%s%s" s1
separator s2)

[<Test>]
let ``should remove last separator from result`` () =
    let data = ["The"; "quick"; "brown"; "fox"; "jumps"; "over";
"the"; "lazy"; "dog"]
    concat " " data |> should not' (endWith " ")

[<Test>]
let ``should clear the string builder before second concatenation`` ()
=
    let data = ["The"; "quick"; "brown"; "fox"; "jumps"; "over";
"the"; "lazy"; "dog"]
    concat " " data |> ignore
    concat " " data |> ignore
    sb.ToString() |> should equal "The quick brown fox jumps over
the lazy dog"
```

The first test will still turn green, but the assumption that it's testing is no longer valid. Since the SUT changed, the test itself no longer provides any value and should be deleted, but because it stays green, it will probably hang around as useless baggage to your test suite.

The second test will break because it has a direct dependency on the implementation detail of the previous SUT. Even though we really didn't change the functionality of the concat function, this test must now be removed in order to run the test suite.

So, if these two seemingly fine tests were wrong, where is the correct abstraction level for our tests?

A beginner's mistake is to implement a function and then decide what to test by looking at the function body. Instead, one should look at the function contract in order to decide what to test. This is where design by contract comes back to us, as we're talking about:

- What the functionality expects
- What the functionality guarantees
- What the functionality maintains

As long as these factors are all maintained, we can make ourselves ensured that the functionality hasn't changed as we keep maintaining the code. Then, how the functionality internally sustains this contract is not that much of an interest to our tests.

Reusing the same SUT, here are some tests that focus on defining from an outside perspective what is expected of the concat function, as follows:

```
[<Test>]
let ``cannot concatenate with null separator`` () =
    raises<exn> <@ concat null ["a"; "b"] @>

[<Test>]
let ``should return empty string for empty list`` () =
    concat " " List.Empty |> should equal ""

[<Test>]
let ``should return item from a one item list`` () =
    concat " " ["a"] |> should equal "a"

[<Test>]
let ``should return concatenated result from string list with empty
separator`` () =
    concat System.String.Empty ["a"; "b"; "c"] |> should equal "abc"

[<Test>]
let ``should be able to form a comma separated value`` () =
    concat ", " ["a"; "b"; "c"] |> should equal "a, b, c"
```

These tests define both what the function expects and what it guarantees, but nothing about what it maintains. The simple reason that functional code seldom maintains any state, and this is not something that we very often have to test for, in contrast to object-oriented code, where maintaining state is a central concept.

It's all about finding and exploring the public interface of the functionality without caring so much about how it is provided. This is where test-first development excels, as we do not know the internals of the implementation before we've started writing the code.

Private functions

Object-oriented programming (OOP) is all about the class exposing a `public` interface toward other classes and keeping its internals `private`. In F#, everything is `public` by default, unless it's a `let` value binding inside a type declaration. Those are `private`.

If we agree that implementation details should not be tested, and `private` methods are implementation details, where does that takes us in F#, where everything is `public` by default? Should we start marking **helper** functions `private` to sort them from the `public` interface we want to expose, or are we just recreating one OOP dysfunction in a functional language?

To a consumer of your interfaces, the `private` functions aren't important, and to a reader of the code, it is not of interest to know what functions are `private`. Instead, it is much more interesting for both consumer and reader to know what functions are `public`.

Signature files to the rescue! We can use these to define what the `public` interface is for a module, and have a clear communication on what to expect from our SUT to the rest of the system. A signature file is simply an F# file with the file `fsi` extension, which defines what members of a namespace or module should be `public`.

The following is a module that defines two operations around prime numbers. It checks if a number is both a prime and a function for extracting all prime factors of a number:

```
module Prime =

    // cache
    let mutable cache = [2]

    // sieve [2..10] -> [2; 3; 5; 7]
    let rec sieve = function
    | [] -> []
    | hd :: tl -> hd :: sieve(tl |> List.filter (fun x -> x % hd > 0))

    // expand [2] 10 -> [2; 3; 5; 7]
    let expand input n =
        let max = input |> List.max
        if n <= max then
            // no expansion
            input
        else
            // expand and recalculate
            input @ [max + 1..n] |> sieve
```

```
// lessThanHalfOf 10 4 -> true
let lessOrHalfOf n = (fun x -> x <= (n / 2))

// returns that n is evenly divisible to number
let evenlyDivisible n = (fun x -> n % x = 0)

// isPrime 13 -> true
let isPrime n =
    // update sieve
    cache <- expand cache (n / 2)
    // not evenly divisible by any number in sieve
    cache
        |> Seq.takeWhile (lessOrHalfOf n)
        |> Seq.exists (evenlyDivisible n)
        |> not

// primeFactors 26 -> [2; 13]
let primeFactors n =
    // update sieve
    cache <- expand cache (n / 2)
    // all evenly divisible by n
    cache
        |> Seq.takeWhile (lessOrHalfOf n)
        |> Seq.filter (evenlyDivisible n)
        |> Seq.toList
```

This code uses a mutable Sieve of Eratosthenes algorithm in order to calculate prime numbers. The sieve is maintained by expanding it whenever necessary. The first time we validate isPrime 1337, it will take 15 milliseconds to calculate the answer, but the next time it will return instantly thanks to the maintained sieve.

There are a lot of helper functions in this module that helps aid in making the actual code more readable, but for as far as the tests are concerned, the only interesting parts are the isPrime and primeFactors functions. In order to communicate this more clearly, we can add a signature file that looks as shown in the following code:

```
module Prime =
    // isPrime 13 -> true
    val isPrime : int -> bool

    // primeFactors 26 -> [2; 13]
    val primeFactors : int -> int list
```

When adding an `fsi` file to your project, make sure it appears before the actual implementation file, or the **fsc** compiler will throw an error that you're adding the same declarations twice.

By defining the signature of what should be `public`, all other definitions in the module become `private` by default. This lets us write tests that focus on the right things:

```
[<Test>]
let ``should evaluate 23 as a prime number`` =
    Prime.isPrime 23 |> should be True

[<Test>]
let ``should evaluate prime factors of 26 as 2 and 13`` =
    Prime.primeFactors 26 |> should equal [2; 13]
```

Encapsulation may not be so strongly advocated in functional programming as it is in object-oriented programming, but it is still highly important for the test you write that you focus on the `public` definition and the contract of the functions instead of the internals of the implementation. This way, you will end up with a test suite that is easily maintained for years to come.

Test doubles

The definition of a test double is a dependency you inject into your program, instead of ordinary functionality, in order to isolate the thing you want to test. We've already seen what you can do by making in-memory versions of your dependencies built in. Sometimes, we want our tests to be able to inject a specific tests dependency that is not built in, and this is where the SUT needs to be extensible enough to allow it.

Just as in C#, we use an interface or abstract class to enable extensibility and allow for dependency injection. To enable this, F# provides us with the ability to implement interfaces using object expressions. This is a great feature for testing.

As an example, lets start with defining an interface. This interface will open a **Comma Separated Value (CSV)** file and allow reading it line by line, as shown in the following code:

```
// loading and processing a csv file line by line
type ICsvReader =
    // open file and return sequence of values per line
    abstract member Load : string -> seq<string list>
```

Here is the real implementation of the interface:

```
// implementation of ICsvReader
type CsvReader () =
```

```
interface ICsvReader with
    member this.Load filePath = seq {
            use streamReader = new StreamReader(filePath)
            while not streamReader.EndOfStream do
                let line = streamReader.ReadLine()
                yield line.Split([|','; ';'|]) |> List.ofSeq
    }
```

This is pretty intuitive. We open up a `StreamReader` class and sequentially read one line at a time until we reach the `EndOfStream` class.

Now, we can use this for reading customers from a file. First, we define the following schema:

```
// schema of the data in csv file
type Customer = { ID : int; Name : string; Email : string;
EnabledSubscription : bool }

// turn the csv schema into Customer records
let schema (record : string list) =
    assert (record.Length = 4)
    let id :: name :: email :: enabledSubscription :: [] = record
    {
        ID = System.Int32.Parse(id);
        Name = name;
        Email = email;
        EnabledSubscription = bool.Parse(enabledSubscription)
    }
```

We use this to turn the CSV result from a `string` list into a `Customer` record. Next, we're ready to read the whole file into `Customer` records, as shown in the following code:

```
// load the whole csv file into list of Customer instances
let getCustomersFromCsvFile filePath (csvReader : ICsvReader) =
    csvReader.Load filePath
        |> Seq.map schema
        |> Seq.toList
```

And, we can easily verify it from F# Interactive.

```
> getCustomersFromCsvFile @"data.txt" (new CsvReader());;

val it : Customer list =
  [{ID = 1;
    Name = "John Doe";
    Email = "john.doe@test.com";
```

```
    EnabledSubscription = true;};
  {ID = 2;
    Name = "Jane Doe";
    Email = "jane.doe@test.com";
    EnabledSubscription = false;};
  {ID = 3;
    Name = "Mikael Lundin";
    Email = "hello@mikaellundin.name";
    EnabledSubscription = false;}]
```

In order to unit test this, we need to exchange the CsvReader for our own implementation that doesn't read from the hard drive. This is where we can use object expressions to simplify our test implementation:

```
[<Test>]
let ``should convert all lines from file into Customers`` () =
    // arrange
    let data = [
            ["1"; "John Doe"; "john.doe@test.com"; "true"];
            ["2"; "Jane Doe"; "jane.doe@test.com"; "false"];
            ["3"; "Mikael Lundin"; "hello@mikaellundin.com"; "False"]
        ]

    // interface implementation by object expression
    let csvReader =
        { new ICsvReader with
            member this.Load filePath = data |> List.toSeq }

    // act & assert
    (getCustomersFromCsvFile "" csvReader).Length |> should equal
data.Length
```

The interesting part here is where the CsvReader is created right in the test and then injected into the getCustomersFromCsvFile file. In C#, this has only been possible with the use of mocking frameworks, but here, it is possible to do directly in the language.

This feature does not completely remove the need of mocking frameworks, as you have to implement the whole interface with object expressions, and this might not always be of interest to the test you're writing.

Dependency injection

What we're used to from object-oriented systems is that dependencies are injected into the classes where they're used. There are a couple of different kinds of injections, namely:

- Constructor injection
- Property injection
- Method injection

Constructor injection is by far the most common injection type in object-oriented programming. This is, of course, in order to make the necessary dependencies mandatory and not have to check if they're set or not.

Here is what constructor injection would look like in F#:

```
type CustomerRepository (csvReader : ICsvReader) =
    member this.Load filePath =
        csvReader.Load filePath
            |> Seq.map schema
            |> Seq.toList
```

The dependency, which here is the ICsvReader, is received in the constructor of the `CustomerRepository` type.

The way to test this is pretty obvious; by creating a test double for the ICsvReader, as seen before, and injecting it into the constructor:

```
[<Test>]
let ``should parse ID as int`` () =
    // arrange
    let data = ["1"; "John Doe"; "john.doe@test.com"; "true"]

    // interface implementation by object expression
    let csvReader =
        { new ICsvReader with
            member this.Load filePath = seq { yield data }}

    // act & assert
    let firstCustomer = CustomerRepository(csvReader).Load("").Item(0)
    firstCustomer.ID |> should equal 1
```

Property injection is often used when the dependency is not mandatory, in order for the class to operate. Another situation when you would use property injection is when you want to simplify the class API and provide default instances but still enable extension by using property injection.

This is what property injection looks like:

```
type CustomerRepository () =
    let mutable csvReader = new CsvReader() :> ICsvReader

    // extension property
    member this.CsvReader
        with get() = csvReader
        and set(value) = csvReader <- value

    member this.Load filePath =
        csvReader.Load filePath
            |> Seq.map schema
            |> Seq.toList
```

This code is discouraged in F#, as it is mutable. In functional programming with F#, we should strive for immutability, and only use mutability for mutable problems and optimizations.

When testing, we need to first create an instance of the `CustomerRepository` type and then exchange the CsvReader for our test double. It requires a bit more ceremony than dealing with the following constructor injection:

```
[<Test>]
let ``should parse EnabledSubscription as bool`` () =
    // arrange
    let customerRepository = CustomerRepository()
    let data = ["1"; "John Doe"; "john.doe@test.com"; "true"]

    // interface implementation by object expression
    let csvReader =
        { new ICsvReader with
            member this.Load filePath = seq { yield data }}

    // exchange internal CsvReader with our test double
    customerRepository.CsvReader <- csvReader

    // act & assert
```

```
let firstCustomer = customerRepository.Load("").Item(0)
firstCustomer.EnabledSubscription |> should be True
```

Method injection in object-oriented programming is simply done by sending the dependency directly to the method as a parameter. This is discouraged in object-oriented programming, as it often is a sign of poor design. In functional programming this is quite a common way of dealing with dependencies, by sending, however, them as an argument to the function shown as follows:

```
type CustomerRepository () =
    member this.Load filePath (csvReader : ICsvReader) =
        csvReader.Load filePath
            |> Seq.map schema
            |> Seq.toList
```

The difference here is that the ICsvReader is sent directly into the Load method:

```
[<Test>]
let ``should parse data row into Customer`` () =
    // arrange
    let data = ["1"; "John Doe"; "john.doe@test.com"; "true"]

    // interface implementation by object expression
    let csvReader =
        { new ICsvReader with
            member this.Load filePath = seq { yield data }}

    // act
    let firstCustomer = (CustomerRepository().Load ""  csvReader).
Item(0)

    // assert
    firstCustomer.ID |> should equal 1
    firstCustomer.Name |> should equal "John Doe"
    firstCustomer.Email |> should equal "john.doe@test.com"
    firstCustomer.EnabledSubscription |> should equal true
```

This concludes how dependency injection in object-oriented programming translates to F#, but in functional programming, there are a couple different approaches when it comes to dealing with dependencies.

Functional injection

The interface declaration is not a functional concept and doesn't really fit into functional programming, but it does lend itself well to present dependency injection in F#. Instead of using the interface to enable extensibility, we should rely on the function signature and use that as the base of the dependency.

Let's continue using the ICsvReader as an example. It really only contains one method, so instead of having an interface, we could resort to its functional signature:

```
string -> seq<string list>
```

Based on that, our implementation would look as follows:

```
let csvFileReader (filePath : string) = seq {
        use streamReader = new System.IO.StreamReader(filePath)
        while not streamReader.EndOfStream do
            let line = streamReader.ReadLine()
            yield line.Split([|','; ';'|]) |> List.ofSeq
    }

// load the whole csv file into list of Customer instances
let getCustomers (getData : string -> seq<string list>) filePath =
    getData filePath
        |> Seq.map schema
        |> Seq.toList
```

Here, we use the function signature, called `csvReader`, as the dependency in the `getCustomersFromCsvFile` file. I have written out the whole function signature here for clarity, but I could remove it all and have the F# compiler discover the type.

The usage then looks as shown in the following code:

```
getCustomers @"data.txt" csvFileReader
```

For testing, we don't have to implement an interface anymore, but can rather just supply a function that matches the function signature of the dependency:

```
[<Test>]
let ``should convert all lines from file into Customers`` () =
    // arrange
    let getData x = seq {
            yield ["1"; "John Doe"; "john.doe@test.com"; "true"];
            yield ["2"; "Jane Doe"; "jane.doe@test.com"; "false"];
            yield ["3"; "Mikael Lundin"; "hello@mikaellundin.com";
"False"]
```

```
        }

    // act & assert
    (getCustomers getData "").Length |> should equal 3
```

This greatly simplified testing with the dependency and made the test more intuitive to read. The risk of using function signatures instead of interfaces is that the SUT might become harder to read and maintain, and you would need to be better disciplined to document what is expected of the dependency.

Currying

When dealing with functional programming, there is a pattern called **currying**, which means we're not supplying all arguments to a function, but are instead receive a function that produces the results with the extra arguments.

Here is a basic example:

```
> let add a b = a + b;;

val add : a:int -> b:int -> int

> let addFive = add 5;;

val addFive : (int -> int)
```

First, we define a function add by adding two numbers together. Then, we send 5 into that function and call it the addFive function. The function signature changes, as we have now supplied one argument, and the new addFive function accepts the other.

This is easier to understand if we expand the function declaration and see what really happens:

```
> let add = (fun a -> (fun b -> a + b));;

val add : a:int -> b:int -> int

> let addFive = (fun b -> 5 + b);;

val addFive : b:int -> int
```

The declarations are exactly the same as before. The let expression is really just syntactic sugar around **lambdas**, as shown here. We can use this to our advantage.

In the following example, I create a compare function for later use when sorting a list of customers by their IDs:

```
    type Customer = {
        ID : int
        Name : string
```

```
}

let compareByID (c1 : Customer) (c2 : Customer) =
    -1 * c1.ID.CompareTo(c2.ID)
```

By using currying, we can, in our tests, verify one function parameter at a time by setting one function parameter to a static value. In this case, I will provide a static `c1` and vary `c2` between my tests. I will do this by a partial application on the `compareByID` parameter:

```
// using currying to set the stage
let compareWithFive customer =
    compareByID customer { ID = 5; Name = "Mikael Lundin' }
```

Now I can use this in my tests:

```
[<Test>]
let ``customer 3 is more than customer 5`` () =
    compareWithFive { ID = 3; Name = "John James" } |> should equal 1

[<Test>]
let ``customer 7 is less than customer 5`` () =
    compareWithFive { ID = 7; Name = "Milo Miazaki" } |> should equal
-1

[<Test>]
let ``customer 5 is equal to customer 5`` () =
    compareWithFive { ID = 5; Name = "Mikael Lundin" } |> should
equal 0
```

This is a very simple technique, albeit a powerful one. We can use currying in order to better communicate the intent of our testing, and by clearly testing one parameter at a time.

Higher order functions

Another technique when testing is to use a higher order function as the dependency. This higher order function would then be replaceable for the test.

In the following example, we use a `getData()` higher order function that in the system will read from a file on the hard drive, but in our test will return an in-memory collection:

```
// return value should match the function signature: unit ->
seq<string list>
let csvFileReader (filePath : string) =
    (fun _ -> seq {
```

```
        use streamReader = new System.IO.StreamReader(filePath)
        while not streamReader.EndOfStream do
            let line = streamReader.ReadLine()
            yield line.Split([|','; ';'|]) |> List.ofSeq
    })

// getData: unit -> seq<string list>
let getCustomers getData =
    getData() |> Seq.map schema |> Seq.toList
```

The usage of this is the beautiful part of it, because it becomes so trivial, as shown in the following:

getCustomers (csvFileReader "")

And now, we can exchange the getData signature part for reading from the database, calling a web service, or using an in-memory test double in our unit tests:

```
[<Test>]
let ``should convert all lines from file into Customers`` () =
    // arrange
    let getData = (fun _ -> seq {
            yield ["1"; "John Doe"; "john.doe@test.com"; "true"];
            yield ["2"; "Jane Doe"; "jane.doe@test.com"; "false"];
        })

    // act & assert
    (getCustomers getData).Length |> should equal 2
```

The difference here is that we don't have to send in an empty string into the getData function, but can apply any kind of argument we wish as long as we adhere to the function signature of the getCustomers function.

Stubbing with Foq

There are two specific types of test doubles, namely stubs and mocks. A stub is a least effort implementation of an abstract class or interface. Sometimes, it is prepared with some stub data, meaning data that is necessary in order to run our tests.

A mock is also a test double, but it will record any interaction and be able to answer asserts on those interactions. You can ask the mock questions such as: was the GetUsers() method called with the ID 42 parameter? And in this way, you can verify the interactions of an isolated unit with its outside world.

There are many .NET mocking frameworks that would work well with F#, like Rhino Mocks, Moq, and NMock. Foq is, however, one framework that is specific to F# and uses its code quotations, as we've already seen with Unquote.

You can install Foq directly to your project from the NuGet Package Manager, as shown in the following screenshot:

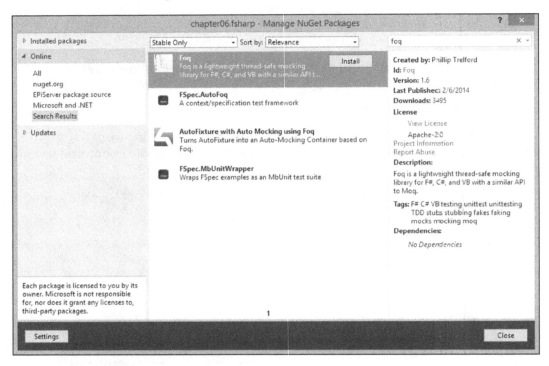

This will add Foq as a reference to your project and you can use it to start writing your first stub.

Let's say we have an interface for managing users in the database, as shown in the following code:

```
type IUserDataAccess =
    abstract member GetUser: int -> User
    abstract member GetUsers: unit -> User list
    abstract member UpdateUser: User -> bool
    abstract member CreateUser: User -> User
    abstract member DeleteUser: int -> bool
```

Using this interface, we want to implement a function to generate a new password for a user. We use the following code:

```
// update a user with new password
let resetUserPassword (dataAccess : IUserDataAccess) user length =
    // define password alphabet
    let alphabet = ['a'..'z'] @ ['A'..'Z'] @ ['0'..'9'] @ ['@'; '$';
'#'; ','; '.']

    // pick random character from alphabet
    let random seed alphabet : char =  List.nth alphabet ((System.
Random(seed)).Next(alphabet.Length))

    // create a string out of random characters
    let password = [for i in 1..length -> random i alphabet]
                    |> List.fold (fun acc value -> sprintf "%s%c" acc
value) ""

    // create new user instance
    let user = {user with Password = password}

    // store user to database and return
    dataAccess.UpdateUser user |> ignore
    user
```

What is interesting for this example is that the code is dependent on the IUserDataAccess method and we're only making use of one method in the interface declaration. If we were to use interface object expression implementation to stub this out, we would have to implement the whole interface, which would get quite messy:

```
[<Test>]
let ``should generate a new password on user`` () =
    // arrange
    let dataAccess =
        { new IUserDataAccess with
            member this.GetUser id = { ID = id; Password = "" }
            member this.GetUsers () = []
            member this.UpdateUser user = true
            member this.CreateUser user = user
            member this.DeleteUser id = true }

    // act
```

```
        let user = resetUserPassword dataAccess { ID = 1; Password = "" }
12

        // assert
        user.Password |> should haveLength 12
```

Instead of using this tedious method, we can generate a stub with Foq, like this.

```
    [<Test>]
    let ``generated password should always be unique`` () =
        // arrange
        let dataAccess =
            Mock<IUserDataAccess>()
                .Setup(fun x -> <@ x.UpdateUser(any()) @>).Returns(true)
                .Create()

        // act
        let user1 =  resetUserPassword dataAccess { ID = 1; Password = ""
} 12
        let user2 = resetUserPassword dataAccess { ID = 2; Password = "" }
12

        // assert
        user1.Password |> should not' (equal user2.Password)
```

The test here is failing, but the interesting thing is to look at how we managed to create a stub with Foq which would only define behavior for one member of the stubbed interface, instead of stubbing out the whole thing.

In this case, we just caught any call to the IUserDataAccess method.UpdateUser and returned true. We could actually set up different return values for different inputs, as shown in the following code:

```
    // delete a list of users
    let deleteUsers users (dataAccess : IUserDataAccess) =
        users
            |> List.map (fun user -> dataAccess.DeleteUser user.ID)
            |> List.zip users
```

This function takes a list of user IDs and deletes the corresponding users from the database. It then reports for each user if the deletion was successful (true) or if it failed (false).

We can easily test this by setting up our stub to return different results depending on the input:

```
[<Test>]
let ``should report status on deleted users`` () =
    // arrange
    let users = [|{ ID = 1; Password = "pass1" };
                 { ID = 2; Password = "pass1" };
                 { ID = 3; Password = "pass1" }|]

    let dataAccess =
        Mock<IUserDataAccess>()
            .Setup(fun da -> <@ da.DeleteUser(users.[0].ID) @>).
Returns(true)
            .Setup(fun da -> <@ da.DeleteUser(users.[1].ID) @>).
Returns(false)
            .Setup(fun da -> <@ da.DeleteUser(users.[2].ID) @>).
Returns(true)
            .Create()

    // act
    let result1 :: result2 :: result3 :: [] = deleteUsers (users |>
List.ofArray) dataAccess

    // assert
    result1 |> should equal (users.[0], true)
    result2 |> should equal (users.[1], false)
    result3 |> should equal (users.[2], true)
```

Foq will record our setup, and when the request comes, it will return the result we have set up for it.

You can also use Foq to verify that your code can handle the edge cases of your integration points, for instance, when the external system throws an exception at you and expects you to catch it:

```
let update (dataAccess : IUserDataAccess) user =
    try
        dataAccess.UpdateUser user
    with
    // user has not been persisted before updating
    | :? System.Data.MissingPrimaryKeyException -> false
```

The `Update` function will handle a `MissingPrimaryKeyException` exception coming from the database:

```
[<Test>]
let ``should return false when updating a user that doesn't exist`` ()
=
    // arrange
    let dataAccess =
        Mock<IUserDataAccess>()
            .Setup(fun da -> <@ da.UpdateUser(any()) @>)
                .Raises<System.Data.MissingPrimaryKeyException>()
            .Create()

    // act
    let result = update dataAccess { ID = 1; Password = "pass1" }

    // assert
    result |> should be False
```

The test shows how we can simulate this by setting up the data access stub to raise the exception, and then expecting it to be handled property in the SUT.

It doesn't get much more complicated than this when stubbing with Foq. The need for stubbing is, in itself, not as great in functional programming as it is in object-oriented, as you can most often extract a dependency by its functional signature instead of having a class for it.

Interfaces should, as a rule, be limited to providing only one service, and having large interface declarations is a code smell. Foq doesn't really come into great use until you have a large interface where you want to stub away only a few of its methods. For those other cases, you're fine just using interface implementation by object expressions.

Mocking

Even though Foq is calling itself a mocking framework, a mock is really a recorder of events on a dependency. You can use it to verify the interactions between parts in your system.

Let's say we have a situation where we want to synchronize customer data from a CRM system onto our local database. We could have interfaces as shown in the following code:

```
type Customer = { ID : int; Name : string }

type ICustomerService =
    abstract member GetCustomers : unit -> Customer list

type ICustomerDataAccess =
    abstract member GetCustomer : int -> Customer option
    abstract member InsertCustomer : Customer -> unit
    abstract member UpdateCustomer : Customer -> unit
```

We write a simple scheduled job that will synchronize data nightly:

```
let synchronize (service : ICustomerService) (dataAccess :
ICustomerDataAccess) =
    // get customers from service
    let customers = service.GetCustomers()

    // partition into inserts and updates
    let inserts, updates =
        customers |> List.partition (fun customer -> None =
dataAccess.GetCustomer customer.ID)

    // insert all new records
    for customer in inserts do
        dataAccess.InsertCustomer customer

    // update all existing records
    for customer in updates do
        dataAccess.UpdateCustomer customer
```

The code itself is pretty straightforward. We extract all customers and split them into two lists, the ones that are going to be inserted, and those that are to be updated. Then, we execute the inserts and updates.

The problem is not a very functional problem, and the solution here is not a pure functional solution, making it hard to test because it doesn't return anything we can assert on.

This is a situation where we would need to use a mock, in order to test the logic. Let's start by adding **RhinoMocks** to our test project, as shown in the following screenshot:

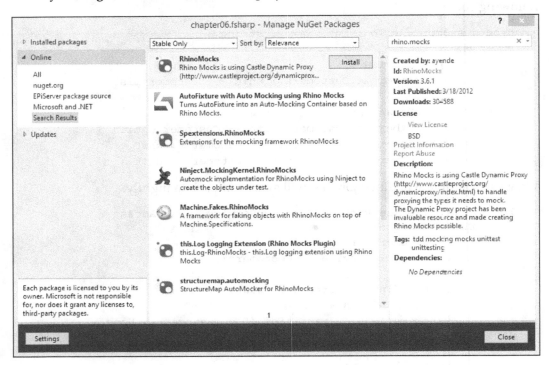

This is a great tool for recording and replaying behavior in your SUT:

```fsharp
open Rhino.Mocks

[<Test>]
let ``should update customers that are already in database`` () =
    // arrange
    let data = [|{ ID = 1; Name = "John Doe" }; { ID = 2; Name = "Jane
Doe" }|]

    let customerService = MockRepository.GenerateMock<ICustomerServi
ce>();
    let customerDataAccess = MockRepository.GenerateMock<ICustomerDat
aAccess>();

    // setup getting data
    customerService.Expect(fun service -> service.GetCustomers()).
Return(data |> Seq.toList);
```

```
    // setup try getting customers from database
    customerDataAccess.Expect(fun da -> da.GetCustomer 1).Return(Some
data.[0])
    customerDataAccess.Expect(fun da -> da.GetCustomer 2).Return(None)

    // act
    synchronize customerService customerDataAccess

    // assert
    customerDataAccess.AssertWasCalled(fun da ->
da.UpdateCustomer(data.[0]))
    customerService.VerifyAllExpectations()
    customerDataAccess.VerifyAllExpectations()
```

Now, this code reads as being very verbose, but it is quite simple in its essence. First, we define some test data where #1 should already exist in the database and #2 should be new.

We put an expectation on the `customerService` function, when it gets a call to the `GetCustomers()` method, it should return our test data.

Then, we put an expectation on the `customerDataAccess` function to define that in #1, there should be a customer returned and in #2, there should be a `None` customer parameter .

We execute the SUT, and lastly, we verify that the `customerDataAccess` function, the `UpdateCustomer()` method was called with the customer that already existed. After that, we call the `VerifyAllExpectations()` method to make sure the expectations we've set up were followed through.

If you would like to go even further, you could use the `MockRepository.GenerateStrictMock` method instead, which is a mock that won't accept any other calls to the mock objects except those you've put expectations on.

For over a year, I thought this was really great stuff, until I started using it in scale. The problem with mocking is that you tend to get very brittle tests. Every time you change an implementation detail, the mocks will break, even if that change didn't affect the `public` interface. Refactoring became very hard and tedious with mock tests breaking, and when a test breaks, though nothing is wrong, it starts costing more in maintenance to justify the value it brings.

The problem is, of course, that the test knows too much about the implementation details, so much that we can't change the implementation details without breaking the test. This is the problem with mocking, just as with `private` members; when the test knows too much about the inner workings of the SUT, they become brittle and costly.

Knowing the dangers of mocking, you should mock in moderation. Test the `public` interfaces, and only put expectations on dependencies when that dependency is a part of the `public` interface. Know the pain to get the gain.

Dealing with databases

The most common question when it comes to unit testing is how to remove the dependency to the database. I have already touched upon a set of techniques on how to use test doubles in order to get around dependencies, but I wanted to use this section of the chapter to take a concrete example of a database and show how to get around it.

When writing code for connecting with a database, I use the convention of isolating all database code within a module and providing that module with a signature file in order to hide its internals.

This will be demonstrated by writing an e-mail queue that is used for storing e-mails in an SQL database before sending them. This is done because the page load of a web application should not have direct dependency on a **Simple Mail Transfer Protocol (SMTP)** server. Instead, e-mails are stored in a table and picked up by a Windows service that will do the sending.

First, you need to add references to the `System.Data`, `Sytem.Data.Linq`, and `FSharp.Data.TypeProviders` namespaces:

```
module EmailDataAccess =

    // insert an e-mail to the database
    val insert : Email -> unit

    // get all queued e-mails from database
    val getAll : unit -> Email list

    // delete an e-mail from the database
    val delete : int -> unit
```

This is the signature file of the database module that we're using to access the database. It should be noted that this is not an interface as in object-oriented programming, but just a `public` definition of the module.

Here is our implementation of the `EmailDataAccess` module:

```
module EmailDataAccess =

    open System
```

```
open System.Data
open System.Data.Linq
open Microsoft.FSharp.Data.TypeProviders
open Microsoft.FSharp.Linq

type dbSchema = SqlDataConnection<"Data Source=.;Initial
Catalog=Chapter04;Integrated Security=SSPI;">
let db = dbSchema.GetDataContext()

// Enable the logging of database activity to the console.
db.DataContext.Log <- System.Console.Out

// insert an e-mail to the database
let insert (email : Email) =
    let entity = new dbSchema.ServiceTypes.Email(
                            ToAddress = email.ToAddress,
                            FromAddress = email.FromAddress,
                            Subject = email.Subject,
                            Body = email.Body)
    db.Email.InsertOnSubmit(entity)
    db.DataContext.SubmitChanges()

// get all queued e-mails from database
let getAll () =
    query {
        for row in db.Email do
        select {
            ID = Some row.ID;
            ToAddress = row.ToAddress;
            FromAddress = row.FromAddress;
            Subject = row.Subject;
            Body = row.Body }
    } |> Seq.toList

// delete an e-mail from the database
let delete id =
    query {
        for row in db.Email do
        where (row.ID = id)
        select row
    } |> db.Email.DeleteAllOnSubmit
    db.DataContext.SubmitChanges()
```

In this implementation, I make sure to hide all the ugliness of the SQL type provider and only expose the `public` definitions we want to make visible. This is often forgotten in functional programming, but very important in terms of maintainability.

Now, we can implement the e-mail queue, like this:

```
module EmailQueue =
    // push e-mails on the queue
    let push (daInsert : Email -> unit) email =
        daInsert email

    // pop e-mail from the queue
    let pop (daGetAll : unit -> Email list) (daDelete : int -> unit) =
        seq {
            for email in daGetAll() do
                daDelete email.ID.Value |> ignore
                yield email
        }
```

It has two functions, `push` and `pop`. The `pop` function will return a sequence of e-mail messages that will be removed from the database as they are retrieved from the sequence. This means if the execution fails in the middle, it won't delete records that haven't been processed, and it will not leave records in the queue that have already been processed. Nice and tidy.

This has no dependency at all to the previously written `EmailDataAccess` library. Instead, we send in the dependencies as functions. Here is a usage example:

```
// push the e-mail
push email EmailDataAccess.insert |> ignore

// pop the e-mail
let popped = pop EmailDataAccess.getAll EmailDataAccess.delete |>
Seq.nth(0)
```

And this makes it trivial to exchange the dependencies and write our unit tests like this:

```
[<Test>]
let ``should delete record when iterating on pop sequence`` () =
    // arrange
    let email = {
            ID = None;
            ToAddress = "hello@mikaellundin.name";
            FromAddress = "hello@mikaellundin.name";
            Subject = "Test message";
```

```
            Body = "Test body"
    }

// stub implementation of EmailDataAccess
let db = System.Collections.Generic.Dictionary<int, Email>()
let insert email = db.Add (0, { email with ID = Some 0 })
let getAll () = db.Values |> Seq.cast<Email> |> Seq.toList
let delete id = ignore <| db.Remove id

// act
push insert email |> ignore
pop getAll delete |> Seq.nth(0) |> ignore

// assert
db.Count |> should equal 0
```

The dependencies are easy enough to stub that we don't need to use an interface implementation, stubbing, or a mocking framework. It's enough to implement some functions that match the functional signature of what we're depending on.

Summary

In this chapter we've learned how to write unit tests by using the appropriate tools to our disposal: NUnit, FsUnit, Unquote, and Foq. We have also learned about different techniques for handling external dependencies, using interfaces and functional signatures, and executing dependency injection into constructors, properties, and methods. Finally, we talked about test doubles, stubs, and mocks and the reasons for avoiding mocking, even in situations where it would seem tempting.

In the next chapter, we will learn about integration testing, when and what to integration test, and how to prepare test data for integration testing. We will test databases and web services and dive into the level of investment that needs to be done in the external system we're testing against.

5
Integration Testing

If unit testing is a way of driving the design of your code, integration testing is purely focused on verifying that your code is working as expected. In this chapter, we will focus on how to use F# for integration testing, touching on the following subjects:

- Writing good integration tests
- Setting up and tearing down databases
- Speeding up integration testing
- Testing stored procedures
- Testing web services

After reading this chapter, you will know how to produce high-quality integration tests that will help you improve your system's stability and verify the contracts to external systems.

Good integration tests

An integration test is a black box test where we try to verify that the different parts of a system work well together. These parts can be different parts that you've developed yourself or integration of databases and web services.

Where the unit test focuses on testing the isolated unit, the integration test will touch upon a larger amount of code and essentially test the system as a whole. In unit testing, we go to a great extent of removing external dependencies, such as web services, databases, and filesystem, from the testing itself. In integration testing, we work to include these dependencies, which will provide the following effects:

- We'll find where our code crashes because of unexpected results from the external system
- Integration tests are usually slower because they are I/O-bound
- Integration tests are brittle because they depend on the filesystem and network

The risk of external systems is that they provide results that are not expected. These results will not be found in unit testing, as you only test for expected errors and not for unexpected errors. Integration testing gives you the ability to find unexpected errors before you start debugging the code or functionally test it.

A program that is pure, without side effects, is an imaginary thing; however, if it did exist, it would not need any integration tests as all states could be found with unit testing alone. Alas! A pure program will not permit dependency on any external state, such as database, filesystem, or console I/O. But if you have a program that is not pure, you need integration testing to find the culprits in your code, where external dependency provides results for what your code was not written for.

You run your unit tests often, and this is because they are fast. There are even tools such as **NCrunch** that will automatically run your tests in the background as you're writing code, having updated test results for you without you lifting a finger. This is pretty neat. With integration tests, this is impossible as integration tests are usually very slow. With very slow, we're talking about hundreds of milliseconds. This doesn't sound like much, but if you have 1,000 integration tests running at 100 milliseconds each, it will take 100 seconds to execute the tests, not something that you would want to do often.

This means that integration tests aren't run that often. Maybe they are run before every code check in, if the developer is disciplined. It is run on the build server, but then the faulty code has already been committed to the version history. I have seen integration test suites that took 5 hours to run and were run only nightly. In the morning, the developers would come in and get the results from the nightly build.

This is of course a downside of integration tests.

Another downside is that integration tests are brittle. There is not much we can do about this because it's the nature of these tests:

- They are bound by the filesystem, so they require that a space be left on the device
- They are bound by the network, so they require the Ethernet/Wi-Fi to work

Many integration tests work with state by setting it up before the test runs and tearing it down when the test run is completed. Two such simultaneous test runs will affect each other states' and fail because of it. This will happen often in a team of 10 developers and one integration server. Your integration tests will fail, and it will not be because your code is broken. It is because the circumstances in which your test is run are bad, and if they were good, the tests would pass. With all this in mind, we need to think about what constitutes an integration test and when the value of this test is greater than the cost? How can we write good integration test suites?

Layer-for-layer testing

One way to do integration testing is to approach the problem in a layer-for-layer way. This way, you will try your external dependency at several levels of your system. The effect is that you'll get granular error messages that will be easy to follow up and fix.

The following image illustrates how to write layer-for-layer tests:

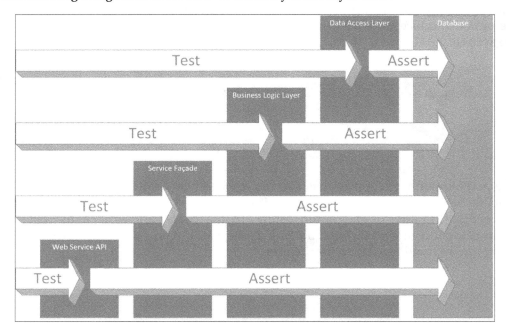

The first test will call the **Data Access Layer** (**DAL**) directly and find problems with the integration between the data access layer and the database. The next test will run against the **Business Logic Layer** (**BLL**) and find problems with the data from the database in the BLL The test on the service facade will find problems that the database may cause in that layer and the test to the web service API, which is the same for that layer.

A novice would point out that only the first test is needed, where testing is done directly on the data access layer, but a seasoned programmer would know that these abstractions are leaky and unexpected null values from the database might just happen to turn up a lot of troubles when serializing the same data to XML in the web service API.

These are the things that layer-for-layer testing will help you to find. The downsides are, of course, that you will pay for your granularity with a lot of redundancy. With redundancy comes high maintenance and slow test suites.

Top down testing

In top down testing, we treat the system as a black box and call only on the external interfaces. We ignore what is inside the box and care only about the result that we will get on our function calls. These calls could be made to a REST service or an assembly, or an HTTP call could be made to a web application. What matters is that we abstract away the internals of the system, and this way, gain in flexibility of that implementation. If the implementation changes, the tests will remain solid, as long as the public interface stays the same. In top down testing we call only the public API of the system:

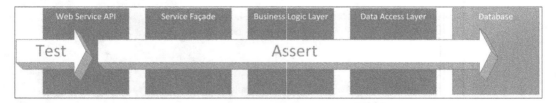

The problem with this approach is that our tests will very rarely be able to specify what went wrong. Sure, it will say what it expected and what result it got instead; however, the failures of integration testing are unexpected and as such unexpected errors seldom come out through the public interface but are cached somewhere along the way and beautified for the user.

The result is a test suite that is very hard to read when it fails, and most often, you will have to dive into the log files in order to find the original exception that caused the error. This is very time consuming, and errors from these tests will consume much more time in troubleshooting than layer-for-layer tests. However, they will be faster to write and easier to maintain.

External interface testing

The last way to write these tests is to only test the actual external interface to the dependency. If the dependency is a database, we only test the actual query to the database and leave all the other layers alone, trusting our abstractions. This is a very efficient way of providing value to the development process very fast, by quickly ruling out the errors in the data access layer and leaving other errors for different kinds of testing, such as functional testing. External interface testing runs the minimal amount of code needed to test the integration:

The reason to do this is that, it is cheap and has a high payback, but we will miss bugs that we need to be ready to deal with in some other way. Sometimes this is quite enough and provides the amount of quality assurance for the effort we're willing to spend, and at other times, we need to go all the way.

Your first integration test

Writing your first integration test is deceivingly easy. You just call your code without caring about the external dependencies, as we do with unit testing.

We have some code that can get user information from the database by the `UserName` parameter:

```
module DataAccess =
    open System
    open System.Data
    open System.Data.Linq
    open Microsoft.FSharp.Data.TypeProviders
    open Microsoft.FSharp.Linq
```

```
    type dbSchema = SqlDataConnection<"Data Source=.;Initial
Catalog=Chapter05;Integrated Security=SSPI;">
    let db = dbSchema.GetDataContext()

    // Enable the logging of database activity to the console.
    db.DataContext.Log <- System.Console.Out

    type User = { ID : int; UserName : string; Email : string }

    // get user by name
    let getUser name =
        query {
            for row in db.User do
            where (row.UserName = name)
            select { ID = row.ID; UserName = row.UserName; Email =
row.Email }
        } |> Seq.tryFind (fun _ -> true)
```

We can write a test like this to verify its functionality:

```
[<Test>]
let ``should return user with email hello@mikaellundin.name when
requesting username mikaellundin`` () =
    // act
    let user = getUser "mikaellundin"

    // assert
    user |> Option.isSome |> should be True
    user.Value.Email |> should equal "hello@mikaellundin.name"
```

This test will turn green because this user exists in the database. But writing a test that depends on a particular state in the database is a particularly bad idea. At some time in the future, the test will fail because the user is no longer in the database. Instead, we should decouple the integration test from the actual state and set up the state that we need before testing and tear it down right after our test is finished:

```
[<Test>]
let ``should be able to retrieve user e-mail from database`` () =
    let dbUser = new dbSchema.ServiceTypes.User(ID = -1, UserName =
"testuser", Email = "test@test.com")

    // setup
    db.User.InsertOnSubmit(dbUser)
    db.DataContext.SubmitChanges()

    // act
```

```
let user = getUser dbUser.UserName

// assert
user |> Option.isSome |> should be True
user.Value.Email |> should equal dbUser.Email

// teardown
db.User.DeleteOnSubmit(dbUser)
db.DataContext.SubmitChanges()
```

We're inserting a new user, a test record, and we're assigning a negative Primary Key ID (PKID) to it so it won't conflict with the real data. After inserting it, we run the test and assert it; then, at last, we remove the test record.

This works well in the happy case. When the test fails, however, it will leave a test record in the database, and the next time the test is run, it will be unable to insert a test record, as the test record is already there. As the test is not thread safe, it will easily fail when two developers run the test suite at the same time:

```
[<Test>]
let ``should be able to get username from database`` () =
    let dbUser = new dbSchema.ServiceTypes.User(ID = -1, UserName =
"testuser", Email = "test@test.com")

    // setup
    db.Connection.Open()
    let transaction = db.Connection.BeginTransaction(isolationLevel =
IsolationLevel.Serializable)
    db.DataContext.Transaction <- transaction
    db.User.InsertOnSubmit(dbUser)
    db.DataContext.SubmitChanges()

    try
        // act
        let user = getUser dbUser.UserName

        // assert
        user |> Option.isSome |> should be True
        user.Value.UserName |> should equal dbUser.UserName

    finally
        // teardown
        transaction.Rollback()
        db.Connection.Close()
```

The code is not that simple anymore, but now the whole integration test is running in a transaction that is rolled back at the very end independent of whether the test succeeds or fails. We have also protected ourselves from concurrent runs by using the `IsolationLevel.Serialize` interface, which will place a lock on the database table until the test is finished. This means if any other test suite runs at the same time, it will have to wait until this test finishes, avoiding the concurrency issue.

Sadly, not many integration tests in the real world are as simple as this one, as the data is dependent on relations to other records and lookup tables that require you to insert a whole graph of data before being able to do the actual testing.

Setting up and tearing down databases

When you're working in a greenfield project and have a favorable situation of designing a database from the ground up, you have complete control over your database when it comes to integration tests, if you do it correctly.

While working on a greenfield project where database development is part of the project, you should adopt fluent migrations as a part of the development cycle. Writing change scripts for database changes has been around for a very long time, but it was Ruby on Rails that popularized migrations as a part of the software development lifecycle, and this has been adopted by .NET in the `FluentMigrator` library.

Let's start by adding a reference to the `FluentMigrator` library in our project:

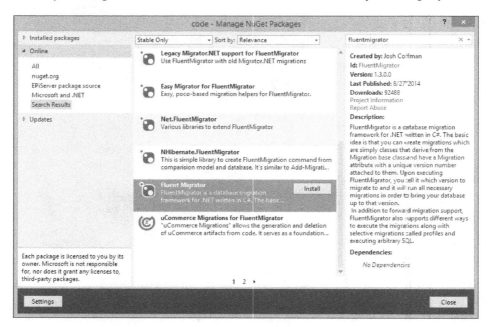

Now we can write our first migration:

```
open FluentMigrator

type Email = { FromAddress : string; ToAddress : string; Subject :
string; Body : string }

[<Migration(1L)>]
type CreateEmailTable () =
    inherit Migration()

    let tableName = "Email"

    override this.Up () =
        ignore <| this.Create.Table(tableName)
            .WithColumn("ID").AsInt32().NotNullable().PrimaryKey().
Identity()
            .WithColumn("FromAddress").AsString().NotNullable()
            .WithColumn("ToAddress").AsString().NotNullable()
            .WithColumn("Subject").AsString().NotNullable()
            .WithColumn("Body").AsString().NotNullable()

        ignore <| this.Insert.IntoTable(tableName)
            .Row({ FromAddress = "test@test.com";
                   ToAddress = "hello@mikaellundin.name";
                   Subject = "Hello";
                   Body = "World" })

    override this.Down () =
        ignore <| this.Delete.Table(tableName)
```

What we see here is an implementation of the `Migration` abstract class. It overrides two methods `Up()` and `Down()`, where the `Up()` method specifies what will happen when migrating to this migration and the `Down()` method specifies what happens when demigrating from this migration.

The attribute on the class has a number that defines in what order this migration should be run. If we call the migration framework with the number 1, the table will get created, and if we call the migration framework with the number 0, the table will be deleted.

After working on the project for a while, we will have a complete set of migrations that will successfully build the database from scratch. We can use this when running our integration tests.

Now you can use the `FluentMigrator` library to create the database from scratch for your test suite:

```fsharp
open FluentMigrator
open FluentMigrator.Runner
open FluentMigrator.Runner.Initialization
open FluentMigrator.Runner.Announcers

// sharing database name between tests

let mutable dbName = ""

type MigrationOptions () =
    interface IMigrationProcessorOptions with
        member this.PreviewOnly = false
        member this.Timeout = 60
        member this.ProviderSwitches = ""

let connectionString dbName = sprintf "Data Source=.;Initial
Catalog=%s;Integrated Security=SSPI;" dbName

[<TestFixtureSetUp>]
let ``create and migrate database`` () =
    // constants
    dbName <- sprintf "Chapter05_%s" (System.DateTime.Now.
ToString("yyyyMMddHHmm"))

    // create database
    use connection = new System.Data.SqlClient.
SqlConnection(connectionString "master")
    use createCommand = new System.Data.SqlClient.SqlCommand("CREATE
DATABASE " + dbName,
connection)
    connection.Open()
    createCommand.ExecuteNonQuery() |> ignore

    // build database from migrations
    let announcer = new TextWriterAnnouncer(System.Diagnostics.Debug.
WriteLine)
    let assembly = System.Reflection.Assembly.GetExecutingAssembly()
    let migrationContext = new RunnerContext(announcer)
    migrationContext.Namespace <- "chapter05"
    let options = new MigrationOptions()
```

```
    let factory = new FluentMigrator.Runner.Processors.SqlServer.
SqlServer2012ProcessorF
actory()
    let processor = factory.Create((connectionString dbName),
announcer, options)
    let runner = new MigrationRunner(assembly, migrationContext,
processor);
    runner.MigrateUp(true);
```

We create a test fixture setup that will run before any of our tests. During development, it is common to share a database between developers to reduce the amount of duplicate work, but when testing, we don't want to run the tests in that same database. Instead, we should have a fixture setup to create a local database on our own machine and build it up using the migrations. This way, we will have a completely fresh database where tests can be run in isolation:

```
[<TestFixtureTearDown>]
let ``drop the database`` () =
    // drop database
    use connection = new System.Data.SqlClient.
SqlConnection(connectionString "master")
    use dropCommand = new System.Data.SqlClient.SqlCommand("DROP
DATABASE " + dbName, connection)
    dropCommand.ExecuteNonQuery() |> ignore
```

The same way, we will have a fixture teardown function that will remove the database when testing is done. We don't want a lot of test databases to hang around on our machine:

```
open System.Data
open System.Data.Linq
open Microsoft.FSharp.Data.TypeProviders
open Microsoft.FSharp.Linq

type dbSchema = SqlDataConnection<"Data Source=.;Initial Catalog=Custo
merRelationsDB;Integrated Security=SSPI;">
let createdb () = let db = dbSchema.GetDataContext(connectionString
dbName)
                  db.DataContext.Log <- System.Console.Out
                  db

let insert (email : Email) =
    let db = createdb()
    db.Email.InsertOnSubmit(new dbSchema.ServiceTypes.
Email(FromAddress = email.FromAddress, ToAddress = email.ToAddress,
Subject = email.Subject, Body = email.Body))
```

```
        db.DataContext.SubmitChanges()

let getFrom fromAddress =
    let db = createdb()
    query {
        for row in db.Email do
        where (row.FromAddress = fromAddress)
        select { FromAddress = row.FromAddress; ToAddress = row.
ToAddress; Subject = row.Subject; Body = row.Body }
    }
```

The important part of SUT is that we can exchange the connection string easily to use the database we have built up for testing. In this code, we can insert new e-mail messages into a database table and search for messages by FromAddress attribute:

```
[<Test>]
let ``can insert into email table`` () =
    // arrange
    let email = { FromAddress = "my@test.com"; ToAddress = "hello@
mikaellundin.name"; Subject = "Test"; Body = "Will be queued for
sending" }

    // act
    insert email

    // assert
    let daEmail = getFrom email.FromAddress |> Seq.nth(0)
    daEmail.FromAddress |> should equal email.FromAddress
    daEmail.ToAddress |> should equal email.ToAddress
    daEmail.Subject |> should equal email.Subject
    daEmail.Body |> should equal email.Body
```

The test is now as naive as we first started out. It can focus on just being a test and verify that the integration with the database works. The setup of the test database and isolation of test data has been taken care of in the test fixture setup and teardown processes.

Even though this procedure seems very costly, running the whole test on my developer machine takes no more than 60 ms. Performance gains come from not having to make calls over the network, but relying on the internal communication on the machine.

The benefits of this method is that you get a completely version-controlled database with migrations that are properly tested before going into production. It moves the development of the database from the **Database Administrator (DBA)** to the application developer, and it allows the developer to test in isolation on his or her own machine. When running tests, there will be no conflict between two developers working together on the same project, as they will run their tests in separate environments. Also, these tests will run quite fast, as they don't have to run over the network.

However, we are dependent on a greenfield database setup, and it only scales up to a level of data and complexity. Once you move into brownfield development, a different set of tools are needed to handle setup and teardown.

Brownfield database setup

Many times when working with databases, we inherit a database that we need to integrate with. We don't have the migration scripts to build the database, and it would be too time consuming to create them in retrospect. What we can do instead is take a backup of the production database and restore it prior to testing.

In order to do this, you need to reference the **Microsoft.SqlServer.Smo** and **Microsoft.SqlServer.SmoExtended** assemblies. They should be in the **Global Assembly Cache (GAC)** if you have a SQL Server installed locally:

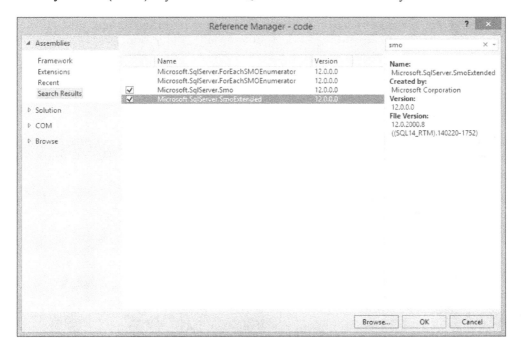

Once we have these references available, we can write a test fixture setup that will restore a database backup prior to our testing using the SMO framework:

```
open NUnit.Framework
open FsUnit

open Microsoft.SqlServer.Management.Smo

let dbFilePath = @"C:\Program Files\Microsoft SQL Server\MSSQL12.
MSSQLSERVER\MSSQL\DATA\"
let dbName = sprintf "Chapter05_%s" (System.DateTime.Now.
ToString("yyyyMMddHHmm"))

[<TestFixtureSetUp>]
let ``Setup database`` () : unit =
    let server = new Server(".")
    server.ConnectionContext.LoginSecure <- true
    server.ConnectionContext.Connect()
    try
        let restore = new Restore()
        restore.Database <- dbName
        restore.Action <- RestoreActionType.Database
        restore.Devices.AddDevice(@"C:\chapter05.bak", DeviceType.
File)
        restore.ReplaceDatabase <- true
        restore.NoRecovery <- false
        restore.RelocateFiles.Add(new RelocateFile("Chapt
er05_201410302303", dbFilePath + dbName + "_Data.mdf"))  > ignore
        restore.RelocateFiles.Add(new RelocateFile("Chapt
er05_201410302303_log", dbFilePath + dbName + "_Log.ldf")) |> ignore
        restore.SqlRestore(server)
    finally
        server.ConnectionContext.Disconnect()
```

This code will open up a connection to the local Microsoft SQL Server and restore a database backup file from the disk. The same way, we can use the SMO framework to delete the database when the test is done:

```
[<TestFixtureTearDown>]
let ``Tear down database`` () : unit =
    let server = new Server(".")
    server.ConnectionContext.LoginSecure <- true
    server.ConnectionContext.Connect()
    try
        server.KillDatabase(dbName)
    finally
        server.ConnectionContext.Disconnect()
```

In my simple database test, it takes no more than 60 ms to perform this, and it will be much more performance efficient than building the migration script history as the database and its complexity grows.

However, this solution is not as clean as the migration setup, as you will bring a backed up state into the test database. This can be good for finding problems when using real data, or bad, if your tests start depending on data that is brought in with the backup.

Really large databases

The tips in the preceding section will work great for small databases. Actually, it will work great for most databases, as you can always strip out the data and just use the schema, which takes very little space at all. Your tests should not depend on the data in the database but only test the integration with the database. For this, you don't need a full set of production data to go along with it.

However, there are situations when it's not probable to work with a stripped-down version of a database, and you need another tactic.

I was working for a client that had a reasonably large database of 50 GB of data. We were doing a heavy amount of testing and the problem we had was to keep an updated version of this data and be able to run integration tests in isolation, as they would fail from time to time when two test suites were run at the same time.

A part of this database was the Swedish national repository for home addresses of all the 10 million residents. We could have cleared the tables of all its data but this would change the prerequisite for the system under test. The database wasn't behaving the same way, with 5 rows of test data compared to 2 million rows of real data, so we decided to leave it in there.

This is not a database that you can easily restore every time you want to run your test suite. Also, the relation tree in the database was quite extensive and you wouldn't want to insert complete sets of test data by code. Instead, we created a stored procedure in the database to set up our test model:

```
CREATE PROCEDURE SetupTestData
AS
BEGIN
    -- SET NOCOUNT ON added to prevent extra result sets from
    -- interfering with SELECT statements.
    SET NOCOUNT ON;

    -- local variables
```

```
DECLARE @PersonID1 int,
        @PersonID2 int,
        @PersonID3 int,
        @AddressID1 int,
        @AddressID2 int;

-- Create test persons
INSERT INTO dbo.Person (SSN, FirstName, GivenName, LastName,
BirthDate)
        VALUES ('193808209005', 'Ingela Ping', 'Ingela', 'Forsman',
'1938-08-20');
    SET @PersonID1 = SCOPE_IDENTITY();

INSERT INTO dbo.Person (SSN, FirstName, GivenName, LastName,
BirthDate)
        VALUES ('194212259005', 'Inge Pong', 'Inge', 'Forsman', '1942-
12-25');
    SET @PersonID2 = SCOPE_IDENTITY();

INSERT INTO dbo.Person (SSN, FirstName, GivenName, LastName,
BirthDate)
        VALUES ('196403063374', 'Jesper', 'Jesper', 'Forsman', '1964-
03-06');
    SET @PersonID3 = SCOPE_IDENTITY();
    -- ... more test persons

-- Create test addresses
INSERT INTO dbo.[Address] (StreetName, StreetNumber, PostalCode,
Town)
        VALUES ('Lantgatan', '38', '12559', 'SOLNA');
    SET @AddressID1 = SCOPE_IDENTITY();

INSERT INTO dbo.[Address] (StreetName, StreetNumber, StreetLetter,
ApartmentNumber, [Floor], PostalCode, Town)
        VALUES ('Stångmästarevägen', '11-13', 'A', '1201', '2',
'15955', 'STOCKHOLM');
    SET @AddressID2 = SCOPE_IDENTITY();
    -- ... more test addresses

-- Create relations
INSERT INTO dbo.NationalRegistrationAddress (Person, [Address],
[Date])
        VALUES (@PersonID1, @AddressID1, '1970-01-01');
    INSERT INTO dbo.NationalRegistrationAddress (Person, [Address],
[Date])
```

```
        VALUES (@PersonID2, @AddressID1, '1970-01-01');
    INSERT INTO dbo.NationalRegistrationAddress (Person, [Address],
[Date])
        VALUES (@PersonID3, @AddressID1, '1970-01-01');
    INSERT INTO dbo.NationalRegistrationAddress (Person, [Address],
[Date])
        VALUES (@PersonID3, @AddressID2, '1982-03-06');
    -- ...more test relations
END
GO
```

Now, we treat the database and all its data as the ground state, and we will not touch or query on that. For all the test data that we need, we add it to this stored procedure. This, however, provides us with a couple of problems:

- You want to insert this data for every test run, but once it is run, the test data will always be there
- It's not isolated; another test can appear and modify this set of data

To solve this, we go back to the beginning of this chapter and look at how to run the setup in a transaction that we will then roll back.

If we have the following system under test:

```
type dbSchema = SqlDataConnection<"Data Source=.;Initial
Catalog=Chapter05;Integrated Security=SSPI;", StoredProcedures = true>
let db = dbSchema.GetDataContext()

// Enable the logging of database activity to the console.
db.DataContext.Log <- System.Console.Out

// get address history of person with ssn number
let getAddressHistory ssn =
    query {
        for addressHistory in db.NationalRegistrationAddress do
        join person in db.Person on (addressHistory.Person = person.
ID)
        join address in db.Address on (addressHistory.Address =
address.ID)
        where (person.SSN = ssn)
        select address
    }
```

This code will return all the addresses that a person has been living at using their **Social Security Number (SSN)**. We do this by simply joining the many-to-many relationship together and querying it on the SSN. This should be no trouble for the database as long as the SSN is indexed properly.

Now, let's write a test that looks as follows:

```
[<Test>]
let ``should get address history from SSN number`` () =
    let ssn = "196403063374"

    // setup
    db.Connection.Open()
    let transaction = db.Connection.BeginTransaction(isolationLevel =
IsolationLevel.Serializable)
    db.DataContext.Transaction <- transaction

    db.SetupTestData() |> ignore // <-- here the db is prepped with
test data

    try
        // act
        let addresses = getAddressHistory ssn |> Seq.toList

        // assert
        addresses.Length |> should equal 2

    finally
        // teardown
        transaction.Rollback()
        db.Connection.Close()
```

Here, we made assumptions on the data in the database, namely on the test data in the stored procedure. It would be optimal to create a module for test data that we could refer to instead of writing out the test data directly in our test, as the data will be under high reuse.

What's happening here is that the test data is inserted by calling the stored procedure, but only in this transaction. The test is run on the transaction, and when the test completes, the transaction is rolled back and no state is changed on the actual tables. This also makes sure that no other test runner can see the data that we're operating on and there will be no conflicts. There might be a performance hit because of the chosen locking mechanism, and you should never try this on a production database.

What we managed to do here is create a sensible integration testing strategy for heavy databases without the problems of persisting state or conflicting test runs. We've found that integration testing looks much easier than it actually is. However, the complexity of an integration test can be mitigated, and in the end, these tests will bring us a lot of value in the long run.

Speeding up integration testing

Integration tests are slow. This is not noticeable when you are at the beginning of the product life cycle and have 50 integration tests, but when you start closing on 1,000 integration tests, they will take a long time to run. This is, of course, because they are I/O-bound, waiting for network traffic.

A unit test should never take more than 10 ms to complete. This means that 1,000 unit tests will run under 10 seconds. This is enough time to make you loose focus but not enough to be called a major hurdle in your work process.

On the other hand, it is not uncommon for an integration test to take 150 ms to complete. If you have 1,000 integration tests, it will take 2–5 minutes to complete the test run. Now, this is a bit optimistic. I had an integration test suite of 850 integration tests running in 18 minutes. Why is this important?

The time it takes to run a test suite will decide whether it will be run or not. When a test suite takes a long time to run, these tests will only be run in the build server where the developer doesn't have to sit around looking at the screen.

As developers aren't running their tests before committing to source control, this means that faulty code will be committed more often and the source control will be in a faulty state. Slow tests are bad and fast tests are good.

Testing in parallel

The most common problem is that our tests are run sequentially and our integration tests spend most of the time waiting on the network.

A query is sent to the database. The test sits around waiting for the database to return a result before it can assert on the expectations. This is a waste and we could definitely speed it up by running tests asynchronously; however, there is no framework available currently that will allow it. Instead, we need to look at running our tests in parallel.

There aren't many frameworks that will allow you to do this. We need to choose between the discontinued MbUnit or version 3 of NUnit, which as of this writing only exists in the alpha release. The FAKE build tool also contains helpers to execute test suites in parallel, but with this, it will also be dependent on tests in different assemblies. It will not parallelize tests in the same assembly.

I chose to write this chapter with the alpha release, looking forward to it being production-ready by the time this book is published.

Let's reuse our previous example with the address register and extend it a little bit:

```
type dbSchema = SqlDataConnection<"Data Source=.;Initial
Catalog=Chapter05;Integrated Security=SSPI;", StoredProcedures = true>

// get address history of person with ssn number
let getAddressHistory ssn (db :
dbSchema.ServiceTypes.SimpleDataContextTypes.Chapter05) =
    query {
        for addressHistory in db.NationalRegistrationAddress do
        join person in db.Person on (addressHistory.Person = person.
ID)
        join address in db.Address on (addressHistory.Address =
address.ID)
        where (person.SSN = ssn)
        select address
    }


let getHabitantsAtAddress streetName streetNumber streetLetter
postalCode (db : dbSchema.ServiceTypes.SimpleDataContextTypes.
Chapter05) =
    query {
        for addressHistory in db.NationalRegistrationAddress do
        join person in db.Person on (addressHistory.Person = person.
ID)
        join address in db.Address on (addressHistory.Address =
address.ID)
        where (address.StreetName = streetName &&
                address.StreetNumber = streetNumber &&
                address.StreetLetter = streetLetter &&
                address.PostalCode = postalCode)
        select person
    }
```

For this, I've written five tests with the following names:

- Should get address history from the SSN number
- Should return empty address history when not found
- Should get all the habitants of the address
- Should get the only habitant of an address
- Should get an empty result of habitants when the address doesn't exist

We're not going into the details of these tests, as I have already described the method, and these are very similar.

When we run these tests in the command line, we will get the following output:

```
Test Run Summary
    Overall result: Passed
  Tests run: 5, Errors: 0, Failures: 0, Inconclusive: 0
    Not run: 0, Invalid: 0, Ignored: 0, Skipped: 0
  Duration: 3.389 seconds
```

These five tests in total take about 3–5 seconds to run. What we can do in this version of NUnit is decorate our tests with the `Parallelizable` attribute. This will enable our tests to run in parallel:

```
[<Test>]
[<Parallelizable(ParallelScope.Self)>]
let ``should get the only habitant of an address`` () =
    let db = dbSchema.GetDataContext()
    db.DataContext.Log <- System.Console.Out

    let streetName, streetNumber, streetLetter, postalCode =
        ("Stångmästarevägen", "11-13", "A", "15955")

    // setup
    db.Connection.Open()
    let transaction = db.Connection.BeginTransaction(isolationLevel =
IsolationLevel.ReadCommitted)
    db.DataContext.Transaction <- transaction

    db.SetupTestData() |> ignore // <-- here the db is prepped
with test data
```

```
        try
            // act
            let persons = getHabitantsAtAddress streetName
    streetNumber streetLetter postalCode db
                            |> Seq.toList
                            |> List.map (fun person -> person.SSN)

            // assert
            Assert.That(persons, Is.EqualTo(["196403063374"]))

        finally
            // teardown
            transaction.Rollback()
            db.Connection.Close()
```

We can also specify the level of parallelization, which means specifying how many threads will run our test by the following assembly attribute:

```
module AssemblyInfo =
    open NUnit.Framework
    [<assembly: LevelOfParallelization(5)>]
    do ()
```

We will see the result when we run the test suite again:

```
Test Run Summary
  Overall result: Passed
 Tests run: 5, Errors: 0, Failures: 0, Inconclusive: 0
   Not run: 0, Invalid: 0, Ignored: 0, Skipped: 0
Start time: 2014-11-04 22:42:41Z
  End time: 2014-11-04 22:42:44Z
Duration: 2.790 seconds
```

The larger the number of tests we have, the larger will be the gain from parallelizing our tests. You will have to make some considerations in case the underlying systems that you're integrating with is serializing your transactions. In this case, the performance might not be gained from parallelizing; you will actually end up with performance that is worse than before.

Testing stored procedures

When talking to developers, many fear and loath the database-stored procedure because they have been told to do so. If you weren't a developer 10 years ago, you won't know where the pain came from. It's not because of the **Transact SQL (T-SQL)** language, which many think is the reason. It's not because of badly written stored procedures because anyone can write bad code in any language. It has to do with DBAs.

The database administrator is the person assigned to be responsible for the database. With this responsibility comes the operational tasks of setting up new databases and validating backups and monitoring them.

A DBA is the owner of the database domain, and as such, he or she wouldn't want developers creating tables, indexes, and such. Instead, the DBA will provide the tables necessary for the developer to store their data. The problem here is that application development and data persistence go hand in hand and need to be done in the same development cycle. However, 10 years ago, database was considered a service, and as such, DBAs provided an API called the stored procedures. This API would let the DBA force constraints on the **callee** and fine-tune permissions at a detailed level. The stored procedure API would entrench the DBA's importance and cause data persistence to become a drag.

The main problem with these stored procedure APIs were that they were an unnecessary abstraction that would only get in the way of application development and be there to create an entrenchment around the DBA's position.

The second problem was that DBAs were seldom programmers themselves and not really fit to produce a well-crafted API. Working with these stored procedures could be challenging at best, and opening up and looking at the implementation would scare most developers dumb.

I think that this structure was hurtful for the software industry, where DBA's evangelized relational databases to be the only data store so they could keep their domain to themselves. When this started to loosen up, other data persistence alternatives quickly came to life. Today, we only see DBAs in large enterprise organizations. In all other cases, operations has taken over the operational tasks of the database and developers happily connect directly to tables without passing through unnecessary layers of abstractions.

Despite its history, the stored procedure is quite a powerful construct to simplify certain tasks within the database, as long as you don't use it to hide business rules that should be expressed in the code.

This example will mimic a simple database table structure for a CMS system:

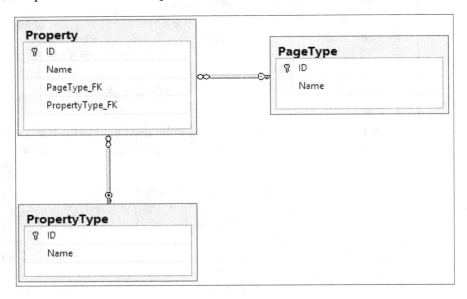

A page in the system, not presented here, has a page type. This page type has properties, and each property is of a specific property type.

Let's populate this table structure with some stub data:

```
[<SetUp>]
let ``insert stub data into cms`` () : unit =
    let db = dbSchema.GetDataContext()

    // truncate the tables
    db.Truncate() |> ignore

    // create page type
    let contentPage = new dbSchema.ServiceTypes.PageType(Name =
"ContentPage")

    // create property types
    let stringPropertyType = new dbSchema.ServiceTypes.
PropertyType(Name = "PropertyString")
    let booleanPropertyType = new dbSchema.ServiceTypes.
PropertyType(Name = "PropertyBoolean")
    let htmlPropertyType = new dbSchema.ServiceTypes.PropertyType(Name
= "PropertyHtml")

    // create properties for content page
```

```
    let pageNameProperty = new dbSchema.ServiceTypes.Property(Name
= "PageName", PageType = contentPage, PropertyType =
stringPropertyType)
    let visibleInMenuProperty = new dbSchema.ServiceTypes.
Property(Name = "VisibleInMenu", PageType =
contentPage, PropertyType = booleanPropertyType)
    let mainBodyProperty = new dbSchema.ServiceTypes.Property(Name
= "MainBody", PageType = contentPage, PropertyType = htmlPropertyType)

    // insert
    db.Property.InsertAllOnSubmit [pageNameProperty;
visibleInMenuProperty; mainBodyProperty]
    db.DataContext.SubmitChanges()
```

As you may have noted, the data inserted was not done in a transaction. Instead, we inserted the data at every test fixture run. In order to do this, we need to truncate the tables in between.

Having the data set up in code might be beneficial if we can make it available to tests that are going to operate on it.

However, we need a `truncate` method, which will remove all the data. This is best done as a stored procedure, so we keep the knowledge of the tables in the same place. The stored procedure to truncate the tables is very simple:

```
CREATE PROCEDURE [Truncate] AS
BEGIN

  DELETE FROM [Property]
  DELETE FROM [PropertyType]
  DELETE FROM [PageType]
END
GO
```

I would call this during the setup of the test and not the teardown, as it could be interesting to look at the database state's post-mortem after a test has failed. If we clear the database after a test is run, we will not have this possibility.

Now we can write a test that verifies the stored procedure works:

```
[<Test>]
let ``truncate should clear all tables`` () =
    // arrange
    let db = dbSchema.GetDataContext()

    // act
    db.Truncate() |> ignore
```

```
// assert
let properties = query { for property in db.Property do select
property } |> Seq.toList
properties.IsEmpty |> should be True

let propertyTypes = query { for propertyType in db.PropertyType do
select propertyType} |> Seq.toList
propertyTypes.IsEmpty |> should be True

let pageTypes = query { for pageType in db.PageType do select
pageType } |> Seq.toList
pageTypes.IsEmpty |> should be True
```

The interesting thing here is that the F# SQL-type provider will generate a function where we can easily call the stored procedure and test it out. We do not have to write any stub code for this, which makes it so powerful.

Let's try a less complicated example and introduce the `Page` and `PropertyValue` tables, which contain the pages that are going to get rendered:

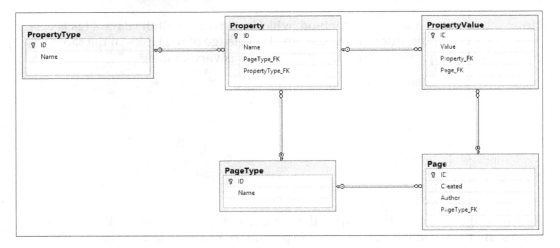

This data model is normalized and a bit hard to work with. Pulling out all pages of a specific type from the data store is not very pleasant and requires a lot of joins. What we can do is define a stored procedure that will help us deliver a denormalized data model:

```
CREATE PROCEDURE GetPagesOfPageType
    @PageType varchar(50)
AS
BEGIN
    SET NOCOUNT ON;
```

```
SET FMTONLY OFF;

DECLARE @Properties varchar(MAX),
        @Query AS NVARCHAR(MAX)


-- extract columns as comma separated string from page type
SELECT @Properties = STUFF(
        (SELECT ',' + property.[Name]
        FROM [Property] property
        INNER JOIN [PageType] pageType ON property.PageType_FK =
pageType.ID
        WHERE pageType.Name = @PageType
        FOR XML PATH('')), 1, 1, '')

SET @Query = N'SELECT pageID, ' + @Properties + N' FROM
    (
        SELECT [page].ID as pageID,
                property.[Name] as name,
                propertyValue.[Value] as value
        FROM [Property] property
            INNER JOIN [PageType] pageType ON property.PageType_FK =
pageType.ID
            INNER JOIN [Page] [page] ON [page].PageType_FK = pageType.
ID
            INNER JOIN [PropertyValue] propertyValue ON propertyValue.
Property_FK = property.ID AND propertyValue.Page_FK = [page].ID
        WHERE pageType.Name = ''' + @PageType + N'''
    ) x

    PIVOT
    (
        max(value)
        FOR name IN (' + @Properties + N')
        ) p'

exec sp_executesql @query
END
```

This stored procedure pivots the data in the columns, so instead of getting a data model that is hard to work with, you will get a result table that is much more normalized and maps better to a model object in the code, as shown in the following image:

	pageID	PageName	VisibleInMenu	MainBody
1	4	Home	true	Welcome to my homepage
2	5	About me	true	I am a software developer
3	6	My Services	true	I build high quality softare in F#

Because this stored procedure returns a dynamic SQL query, the type provider will not be able to pick up the schema automatically. We will need to implement a simple **Object Relational Mapper (OR mapper)** for this:

```
type ContentPage = { pageID : int; PageName : string; VisibleInMenu :
bool; MainBody : string }

// map dataRecord to pageType
let convert<'pageType> (dataRecord : IDataRecord) =
    let pageType = typeof<'pageType>
    let values = FSharpType.GetRecordFields(pageType)
                    |> Array.map (fun field -> Convert.
ChangeType(dataRecord.[field.Name], field.PropertyType))
    FSharpValue.MakeRecord(pageType, values) :?> 'pageType


// get all pages of type
let getPagesOfType<'pageType> (db : dbSchema.ServiceTypes.
SimpleDataContextTypes.Chapter05) =
    seq {
        let command = db.Connection.CreateCommand()
        command.CommandText <- "GetPagesOfPageType"
        command.CommandType <- CommandType.StoredProcedure

        let pageTypeParameter = new System.Data.SqlClient.
SqlParameter("PageType", typeof<'pageType>.Name)
        command.Parameters.Add(pageTypeParameter) |> ignore

        db.Connection.Open()

        try
```

```
        use reader = command.ExecuteReader()
        while reader.Read() do
            yield (reader :> IDataRecord) |> convert<'pageType>

    finally
        db.Connection.Close()
}
```

Here I defined a record type that will act as my page type. I will then define a function called `getPagesOfType` that will retrieve the data as seen in the preceding code and then map that to the record type.

In order to verify that it works, we need to append some data to our `setup` function:

```
// create page function
let createPage created author pageType =
    new dbSchema.ServiceTypes.Page(Created = created, Author = author,
PageType = pageType)

// create property on page
type dbSchema.ServiceTypes.Page with
    member this.addPropertyValue propertyDefinition value =
        this.PropertyValue.Add(new dbSchema.ServiceTypes.
PropertyValue(Value = value, Page = this, Property =
propertyDefinition)) |> ignore
        this

// create pages
let startPage =
    (((createPage DateTime.Now "Mikael Lundin" contentPage)
        .addPropertyValue pageNameProperty "Home")
        .addPropertyValue visibleInMenuProperty "true")
        .addPropertyValue mainBodyProperty "Welcome to my homepage"

let aboutPage =
    (((createPage DateTime.Now "Mikael Lundin" contentPage)
        .addPropertyValue pageNameProperty "About Me")
        .addPropertyValue visibleInMenuProperty "true")
        .addPropertyValue mainBodyProperty "I am a software developer"

let servicesPage =
    (((createPage DateTime.Now "Mikael Lundin" contentPage)
        .addPropertyValue pageNameProperty "My Services")
```

```
        .addPropertyValue visibleInMenuProperty "true")
        .addPropertyValue mainBodyProperty "I build high-quality
software in F#"

// insert
db.Page.InsertAllOnSubmit [startPage; aboutPage; servicesPage]
db.DataContext.SubmitChanges()
```

Here we used the new definitions and added our pages and properties on top of them. Now we're actually ready to see whether this works. Here is our test function:

```
[<Test>]
let ``get all pages of a page type`` () =
    // arrange
    let db = dbSchema.GetDataContext()

    // act
    let page1 :: page2 :: page3 :: [] =
getPagesOfType<ContentPage>(db) |> Seq.toList

    // assert
    page1.PageName |> should equal "Home"
    page1.VisibleInMenu |> should equal true
    page1.MainBody |> should equal "Welcome to my homepage"

    page2.PageName |> should equal "About me"
    page2.VisibleInMenu |> should equal true
    page2.MainBody |> should equal "I am a software developer"

    page3.PageName |> should equal "My Services"
    page3.VisibleInMenu |> should equal true
    page3.MainBody |> should equal "I build high-quality software
in F#"
```

I just love how easy this reads; it hardly needs any explaining at all. In the end, we managed to use F# to test stored procedures, both with the built-in SQL type provider and by calling the stored procedure and mapping it up manually. It is very easy, and there is really no excuse for not testing your database properly.

Data-driven testing

One important aspect when doing integration testing is to be able to test with a diversity of data. This might at times render a lot of repetition, for example, we might want to run the same exact test but with other input values. Instead of writing a unique test for each and every test case, you can write a general test and supply the data for the test separately.

In order to demonstrate this, go back to our address register and query it for addresses. This is what our SUT will look like:

```
type dbSchema = SqlDataConnection<"Data Source=.;Initial
Catalog=Chapter05;Integrated Security=SSPI;">

// find an address by a search string
let searchAddress q (db : dbSchema.ServiceTypes.
SimpleDataContextTypes.Chapter05) =
    query {
        for address in db.Address do
        where ((address.StreetName.StartsWith q) ||
               (address.StreetNumber = q) ||
               (address.PostalCode.StartsWith q))
        select address
    }
```

This function will allow you to search for an address on three different parameters: street name, street number, and postal code. Here, street number must be an exact match, but it's fine for the street name and postal code to match partially.

This requires some extensive testing. Instead of writing all these tests, we can provide one test function with input arguments.

In this example, we supply two arguments to the test function. First is the query that will run and the second is a Boolean argument that specifies whether we can expect the query to find our test address or not:

```
[<TestCase("Lant", true)>]    // match start of street name
[<TestCase("gatan", false)>]  // not matching end of street name
[<TestCase("L", true)>]       // matching single letter
[<TestCase("38", true)>]      // matching whole street number
[<TestCase("3", false)>]       // not matching part of street number
[<TestCase("12559", true)>]   // matching whole postal code
[<TestCase("125", true)>]     // matching start of postal code
[<TestCase("59", false)>]      // not matching end of postal code
let ``should query address register`` q expectedFind =
    // setup
    let db = dbSchema.GetDataContext()
    db.Connection.Open()
    let transaction = db.Connection.BeginTransaction(isolationLevel =
IsolationLevel.Serializable)
    db.DataContext.Transaction <- transaction
```

```
        db.SetupTestData() |> ignore // <-- here the db is prepped with
    test data

    try
        // act
        let addresses = searchAddress q db |> Seq.toList

        // assert
        let found = addresses
                    |> Seq.exists (fun address ->
                        (address.StreetName = "Lantgatan") &&
                        (address.StreetNumber = "38") &&
                        (address.PostalCode = "12559"))

        found |> should equal expectedFind

    finally
        // teardown
        transaction.Rollback()
        db.Connection.Close()
```

This kind of testing is very suitable for certain kinds of problems where you have the same function that you want to try with a range of data.

Testing web services

In this chapter, I have been talking exclusively about databases because database is the most common part of a system where you would want to perform the integration test. The database is often part of your system design and a unit in the solution architecture. Web services are in our architecture just as often internal to our systems as hosted externally by a third party.

This leads us to the question: should we test external web services?

Most of the time, you should not care about testing external services. If there is a well-defined API that feels stable, it is not your responsibility to cover it with tests.

However, if the external API is developed as a part of your solution, there could be a huge benefit for you to write a set of integration tests that will define the contract of what your application is expecting from the API and hand it over to a third party. They can use these tests to verify that your client will work together with their implementation. This way of integrating between teams is extremely powerful.

Another reason for writing tests that hit an external service is to discover the service, figure out how it works, and note the quirks it has before implementing your client. These tests should be inactivated once the client is implemented, as the discovery phase is over and they do not bring value anymore.

You should be really careful when writing integration tests that will hit external services. Always strive for running your tests against a test web service at the receiving end so you don't cause side effects on the production system.

It is also quite common with external web services that they're charged on every API call you make. This could make automation an expensive story, and I would suggest that you really get to bottom of it before you start writing automated tests for external services.

I recommend that you follow the advice of vertical slice testing and implement the external service as an in-memory representation so you can choose not to care about external dependency when you want to test other things. These are the kinds of test harnesses that really pay off once they are in place.

Web service type provider

When working with testing SOAP web services from C#, you need to generate code by creating a client through Visual Studio. In F#, none of this is necessary.

Let's say that we create the following web service:

```
[ServiceContract]
public interface IValidationService
{
    [OperationContract]
    ValidationResult ValidateEmail(string input);
}

[DataContract]
public class ValidationResult
{
    public ValidationResult()
    {
    }

    public ValidationResult(string identifier)
    {
        Identifier = identifier;
    }
```

```
    [DataMember]
    public string Identifier { get; set; }

    [DataMember]
    public ValidationStatus Status { get; set; }

    [DataMember]
    public string ErrorMessage { get; set; }
}

[DataContract]
public enum ValidationStatus
{
    [EnumMember]
    None = 0,

    [EnumMember]
    Valid = 1,

    [EnumMember]
    Invalid = 2,

    [EnumMember]
    Error = 3,
}
```

This is implemented with the following implementation:

```
public class ValidationService : IValidationService
{
    const string EmailValidation = "EmailValidation";
    const string EmailExpression = @"^[A-Z0-9._%+-]+@[A-Z0-9.-]+\.
[A-Z]{2,4}$";

    public ValidationResult ValidateEmail(string input)
    {
        var result = new ValidationResult(EmailValidation);

        try
        {
            var expression = new Regex(EmailExpression, RegexOptions.
IgnoreCase);

            if (expression.IsMatch(input))
            {
```

```
                    result.Status = ValidationStatus.Valid;
                }
                else
                {
                    result.Status = ValidationStatus.Invalid;
                }
            }
            catch (Exception ex)
            {
                result.Status = ValidationStatus.Error;
                result.ErrorMessage = ex.Message;
            }

            return result;
        }
    }
```

When we start the implementation, we will generate a **Web Services Description Language (WSDL)** contract on http://localhost:53076/ValidationService. svc?wsdl. The port number might vary from machine to machine. This is also what we will use in order to generate a type provider for F#:

```
type ValidationService = WsdlService<"http://localhost:53076/
ValidationService.svc?wsdl">

// mapping the generated classes into a discriminated union
type ValidationStatus =
    | Valid
    | Invalid
    | Error of message : string
    static member Create (input : ValidationService.ServiceTypes.
chapter07.code.service.ValidationRe
sult) =
        match input.Status with
        | ValidationService.ServiceTypes.chapter05.code.service.
ValidationSt
atus.Valid -> Valid
        | ValidationService.ServiceTypes.chapter05.code.service.
ValidationSt
atus.Invalid -> Invalid
        | ValidationService.ServiceTypes.chapter05.code.service.
ValidationSt
atus.Error -> Error(input.ErrorMessage)
        | _ -> failwith "Unknown validation status"
```

```
// wrapper that provides a functional interface
let validateEmail (service : ValidationService.ServiceTypes.
SimpleDataContextTypes.ValidationSe
rviceClient) input =
    let result = service.ValidateEmail(input)
    match result |> ValidationStatus.Create with
    | Valid -> true
    | Invalid -> false
    | Error message -> failwith ("Validating e-mail cause
following error: " + message)
```

Let's write tests that will verify that our validation service works:

```
[<TestCase("hello@mikaellundin.name")>]
[<TestCase("mikael.lundin@litemedia.se")>]
[<TestCase("mikael.lundin@valtech.se")>]
[<TestCase("mikael.lundin@litemedia.info")>]
let ``should validate as e-mail address`` (input) =
    // arrange
    let service = ValidationService.GetBasicHttpBinding_
IValidationService()

    // act / assert
    (validateEmail service input) |> should be True


[<TestCase("not an e-mail")>]
[<TestCase("not@email")>]
[<TestCase("not@an@email")>]
[<TestCase("@notanemail")>]
[<TestCase("notanemail@")>]
[<TestCase("@notanemail@")>]
let ``should not match as an e-mail address`` (input) =
    // arrange
    let service = ValidationService.GetBasicHttpBinding_
IValidationService()

    // act / assert
    (validateEmail service input) |> should be False
```

```
[<Test>]
let ``should fail validation with e-mail is null`` () =
    // arrange
    let service = ValidationService.GetBasicHttpBinding_
IValidationService()

    // act / assert
    (fun () -> (validateEmail service null) |> ignore) |> should
throw typeof<System.Exception>
```

The question that comes to mind is whether the value these web service tests are worth the effort and whether we could have achieved the same by testing the `ValidationService()` method directly with a unit test.

What we are testing here is how the client meets the service and how the network and transport parts of this service works together. We have intricate things such as authentication, authorization, and transport security to deal with—all that you will be happy to have tested out before deploying an SSL WCF service to production.

Summary

In this chapter, we learned about how to write integration tests and what constitutes a good integration test. We have been testing databases and dealing with their setups and teardowns. We looked at how to write tests for a web service in order to verify the complete system and its integration.

In the next chapter, we will get into a bird's-eye perspective and do black box testing, as if we didn't know about its internals. We will do this by learning some tools that will help us drive web browsers, query HTML, and express tests in a format that even your manager will appreciate.

6
Functional Testing

Functional testing involves testing the function of a program. It's a higher form of abstraction than the testing we have done so far, as it is a black box test and we don't care about the internal workings of our program, only that it delivers the expected results.

In this chapter, we will learn about the following topics:

- What functional testing is and how to apply it
- Writing executable specifications with TickSpec
- Wielding a web browser as a testing tool
- Which tests provide the best regression for our application

Functional testing is a practice with many names and is often confused with manual testing. This is because what testers do is functional testing, even though they are doing it manually. In order to ensure the quality of the system, testers will verify the functionality with the specification. I've heard of testers that use automated tests to ensure they have regression in their testing, without having to repeat the same testing task over and over again. This makes functional testing not only a development task, but also a common task for testers and developers alike.

Specifications

I hear very often when coaching teams that, we are doing agile so we don't write specifications.

One of the most common misconceptions around agile testing is that you do not create any documentation. This is because the main principal working software for comprehensive documentation is often misinterpreted as "do not write documentation." They're missing the whole point of the agile manifesto, where there is value in the items on the right; however, we value the items on the left more.

Agile testing is striving for a learning process in which you can adapt to it through a software development process. The error in the waterfall procedure is in trying to specify everything from the beginning because we can't know everything from the start. The domain is too complex, and we need to break it down into chunks and start with the most important ones. Once we've done this, we will also have learned new things that will let us re-evaluate how to tackle the rest of the problem, and this is true until the project ends.

Specifications are crucial for development in order to know when you're done, but they are also crucial for functional testing because the specification will be your answer if the feature is correctly implemented. You do not specify the whole system at the start of the project. Instead, you should have a dedicated tester on your team that will specify the most prioritized product backlog items so they're ready when it's time for sprint planning. This will also make committing user stories to the sprint much easier.

Before the work is begun, the functionality is specified. After the work has been completed, the functionality is verified according to its specification. And after the functional tests have been written, the specification can be thrown away.

Setting up TickSpec

TickSpec is a lightweight **Behavior-driven Design** (BDD) framework for F#, influenced by SpecFlow from C#, which has its root in the Ruby testing framework, Cucumber. What is common between all these frameworks is that they implement a domain specific language called **Gherkin**, which is used to express the tests.

Let's start by adding **TickSpec** from the **NuGet package manager** to our application, as shown in the following screenshot:

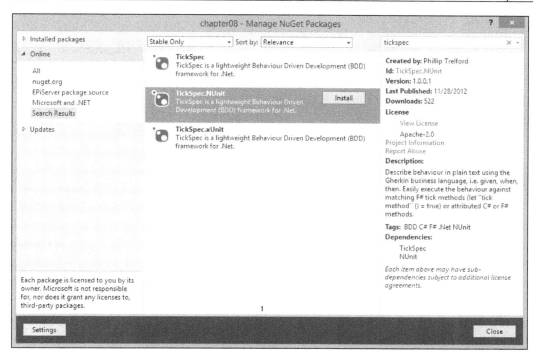

Next up, we will write our first feature file. This file will specify what we expect of the feature and provide scenarios for us to verify. This file is written in Gherkin DSL to mimic the natural language.

Here is a feature file for Conway's Game of Life:

```
Feature: Conway's Game of Life


Scenario 1: Any live cell with fewer than two live neighbors dies, as
if caused by under-population.
   Given a live cell
   And has 1 live neighbor
   When turn turns
   Then the cell dies


Scenario 2: Any live cell with two or three live neighbors lives on to
the next generation.
   Given a live cell
   And has 2 live neighbors
   When turn turns
```

```
    Then the cell lives


    Scenario 3: Any live cell with more than three live neighbors dies, as
    if by overcrowding.
        Given a live cell
        And has 4 live neighbors
        When turn turns
        Then the cell dies


    Scenario 4: Any dead cell with exactly three live neighbors becomes a
    live cell, as if by reproduction.
        Given a dead cell
        And has 3 live neighbors
        When turn turns
        Then the cell lives
```

The magic words in each scenario are Given, When, and Then. This structure set up the user case we wanted to test. They were also mapped to definitions written in F# that specify how each of the Given, When, and Then words should be interpreted.

Even though the code definition looks like plain English, it is written in a format we have decided will be easy for F# definitions to interpret and lend itself well for reuse.

Let's look at the code definitions:

```fsharp
module GameOfLifeDefinitions

open TickSpec
open NUnit.Framework
open Microsoft.FSharp.Reflection

open GameOfLife

let mutable cell = Dead(0, 0)
let mutable cells = []
let mutable result = []

let [<Given>] ``a (live|dead) cell`` = function
    | "live" -> cell <- Live(0, 0)
    | "dead" -> cell <- Dead(0, 0)
    | _ -> failwith "expected: dead or live"

let [<Given>] ``has (\d) live neighbors?`` (x) =
```

```
        let rec _internal x =
            match x with
            | 0 -> [cell]
            | 1 -> Live(-1, 0) :: _internal (x - 1)
            | 2 -> Live(1, 0) :: _internal (x - 1)
            | 3 -> Live(0, -1) :: _internal (x - 1)
            | 4 -> Live(0, 1) :: _internal (x - 1)
            | _ -> failwith "expected: 4 >= neighbors >= 0"
        cells <- _internal x

    let [<When>] ``turn turns`` () =
        result <- GameOfLife.next cells

    let [<Then>] ``the cell (dies|lives)`` = function
        | "dies" -> Assert.True(GameOfLife.isDead (0, 0) result, "Expected
cell to die")
        | "lives" -> Assert.True(GameOfLife.isLive (0, 0) result,
"Expected cell to live")
        | _ -> failwith "expected: dies or lives"
```

Here, we find the words Given, When, and Then again. Instead, it specifies how the keyword should be interpreted. In the first example, we mapped the following:

- Given a live cell
- Given a dead cell

In the function names, we allow regular expressions in order to match more than one exact statement from the specification. So, when we create a match such as the [<Given>] ``a (live|dead) cell`` function, it will match both the Given statements from the specification.

Using regular expressions, we can use the same implementation for both live and dead values, and this makes the definition reusable.

In the next example, we will match the number of live numbers that are given. This will quickly reveal why I chose to write a number instead of the words one, two, or three, which would sound more like natural English, but be harder to interpret.

The function recursively builds the test domain by calling itself with a decremented number of neighbors every time.

The When clause is meant to execute the test the same way as in our previous test pattern. Then asserts that the result was expected.

Next, we need to tie it together with NUnit so it becomes a proper test. This comes directly from the example code by Phil Trelford that is installed together with the TickSpec package:

```
module NUnit.TickSpec

open NUnit.Framework
open System.IO
open System.Reflection
open TickSpec

let assembly = Assembly.GetExecutingAssembly()
let definitions = new StepDefinitions(assembly)

/// Inherit from FeatureFixture to define a feature fixture
[<AbstractClass>]
[<TestFixture>]
type FeatureFixture (source:string) =
    [<Test>]
    [<TestCaseSource("Scenarios")>]
    member this.TestScenario (scenario:Scenario) =
        if scenario.Tags |> Seq.exists ((=) "ignore") then
            raise (new IgnoreException("Ignored: " + scenario.Name))
        scenario.Action.Invoke()
    member this.Scenarios =
        let s = File.OpenText(Path.Combine(@"..\..\",source))
        definitions.GenerateScenarios(source,s)

type Feature () = inherit FeatureFixture("GameOfLifeFeature.txt")
```

This will generate NUnit tests for the scenarios. After compiling the tests, you will see the following in your **Test Explorer** window (or any other chosen test runner):

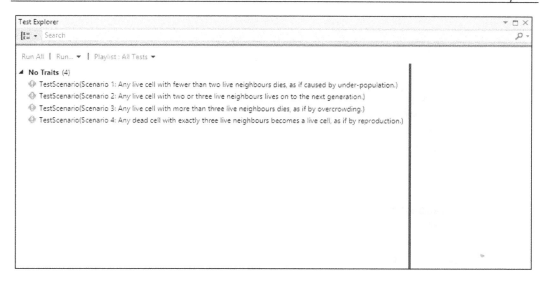

These tests will now fail until we have implemented the actual Game of Life. This implementation could look something like this:

```
module GameOfLife

type Cell = | Dead of x : int * y : int | Live of x : int * y : int

// get coordinate from a cell
let coord = function | Live(x, y) -> x, y | Dead(x, y) -> x, y

// get if the cell on the coordinate is live
let isLive coordinate cells =
    cells |> List.exists (fun cell -> cell |> coord = coordinate)

// get if the cell on the coordinate is dead
let isDead coordinate cells =
    not (isLive coordinate cells)


let live = function Live(_,_) -> true | _ -> false
let dead = function Dead(_,_) -> true | _ -> false
```

```
// get all surrounding cells
let neighbors (cell : Cell) cells =
    let x, y = cell |> coord
    let neighbors = [(x, y - 1); (x, y + 1); (x - 1, y); (x + 1, y)]

    neighbors
    |> List.map(fun coord ->
        match isLive coord cells with
        | true -> Live(coord)
        | false -> Dead(coord))

// is list length less than n
let moreThanOneLessThanThree (list : 'a list) =
    list.Length > 1 && list.Length < 4

// get the next play board
let next (cells : Cell list) =
    printfn "%A" cells
    // Scenario 1: Any live cell with fewer than two live neighbors
dies, as if caused by under-population.
    // Scenario 3: Any live cell with more than three live neighbors
dies, as if by overcrowding.
    let oldCells =
        cells
        |> List.filter (fun cell -> (neighbors cell cells) |> List.
filter live |> moreThanOneLessThanThree)

    // Scenario 4: Any dead cell with exactly three live neighbors
becomes a live cell, as if by reproduction.
    let newCells =
        cells
        |> List.collect(fun cell -> neighbors cell cells)
        |> List.filter dead
        |> List.filter (fun cell -> neighbors cell cells |> List.
filter live |> List.length |> ((=) 3))
        |> List.map (fun cell -> Live(cell |> coord))

    oldCells @ newCells
```

This is one way to implement Conway's Game of Life, but there are many implementations out there that are much more efficient than this one.

Executable specifications

The executable specification is somewhat a mystery, as it often falls between the chairs. It's not picked up by developers because it operates on an abstraction level that is not attractive to them. It also doesn't work as a design tool as unit testing does.

It may, however, be a very useful tool for any tester that is ready to write some code. Sure, the executable specification reads well in plain English, but you will never have product owners writing executable specifications that will just work or even be the base for the implementation.

Instead, the most useful task for executable specifications is for the product owner and team to find a common ground where they can talk about such specifications. The product owner will drive the requirements for the specifications of the functionality, and the developers will put these in a format that can be made into executable specifications. This is where you will find that executable specifications become a very powerful collaboration tool.

In order to get a good test suite, you will have to write high-quality feature files. There are some criteria you should consider when working on feature files:

- Let it be about the feature and not about the system
- It's a specification, and not a test script
- A scenario should test only one thing
- It should be short and concise
- Scenarios should be easy to access

You might want to go to the feature files in order to find out what is expected of a feature. This puts very high requirements on the quality of those feature files. If they are full of repetition or are long and tedious, they will not be used as the main source for the specification documentation.

The typical anti-patterns of feature files are as follows:

- Long sentences
- Repetitive sentences or scenarios
- Repetitive use of "and" to check just one more thing

Try to write the feature files as if they were written in plain English, even if there is a format enforced. With this, we should be able to write feature files that are easy and fun to read, and we could begin by reading them to ourselves in order to achieve this.

Scenarios that are the same from one another with just a few variables swapped out are not easy to read and will not be used as active documentation. If there is repetition, one can use a table in order to bake those scenarios into one:

```
Feature: Contact form

Scenario: Both e-mail fields must add up
    Given I have entered the following into the contact form
    | Name   | Email1         | Email2        | Phone   | Message |
    | Mikael | hello@test.com | hey@test.com  | 5551234 | Eello   |
    When submitting the form
    Then I should be informed of mismatching e-mail addresses
```

Even if very few definitions in this feature will be reusable, it reads better to put data like this in a form.

When you have a lot of setup to do for these scenarios, they can be expressed as the background of your feature:

```
Background:
    Given a global administrator named "Greg"
    And a blog named "Greg's anti-tax rants"
    And a customer named "Dr. Bill"
    And a blog named "Expensive Therapy" owned by "Dr. Bill"
```

This example, taken from the SpecFlow documentation, shows how to properly set up the prerequisites for the scenarios, removing this repetition from each scenario in the feature file.

Of course, the great thing about executable specifications that we never must forget is that its documentation will never become obsolete. Once you change the feature without updating the specification, the tests will break.

Combinatorial examples

One of the more powerful features of executable specifications is the combinatorial example, which lets you use examples as input for your test. In the same manner as NUnit test cases, this allows you to write one test case and verify it with a good amount of different data:

```
Feature: Sign up form

Scenario: E-mail registration should only accept valid addresses
    Given I've entered my name and agreed to terms and conditions
    When I enter <email> into the e-mail field
    Then the page should let me know the registration was <success>

Examples:
    | email                          | success |
    | hello@mikaellundin.name        | true    |
    | hello.you@mikaellundin.name    | true    |
    | hey@litemedia.se               | true    |
    | invalid                        | false   |
    | @mikaellundin.name             | false   |
    | hello.you.mikaellundin.name    | false   |
    | hey@litemedia                  | false   |
```

Here, we wanted to verify a registration form on a web page by sending in a couple e-mail addresses. We did not specify what the system would do depending on the result, only that the system would give some kind of feedback through which we would determine whether the e-mail address was accepted or not. Our test isn't really affected if we get an error page or error message by AJAX.

Here, I have implemented the definitions file to match the examples and pick them up in our tests:

```
module SignUpDefinitions

open TickSpec
open NUnit.Framework

let [<Given>] ``I've entered my name and agreed to terms and
conditions`` () =
    // shortened for brewity: setup
    ()

[<When("I enter {0} into the e-mail field", "(.*?)")>]
let [<When>] ``I enter (.*?) into the e-mail field`` (email : string)
=
    // shortened for brewity: write the e-mail into the field on the
page
```

```
printf "%A" email

[<Then("the page should let me know the registration was {0}",
"(true|false)")>]
let [<Then>] ``the page should let me know the registration was
(true|false)`` (success : bool) =
    // shortened for brewity: verify what the system did after
entering e-mail
    if success then
        Assert.True(success);
    else
        Assert.False(success);
```

The first thing you will notice as strange is the double attributes on `When`/`Then`. The first attribute will match the data from the table with the test, and in that sense, generate the tests that will run.

The second attribute is the same as our previous example: mapping the input data to the arguments of the function.

When we run this, it almost looks like magic:

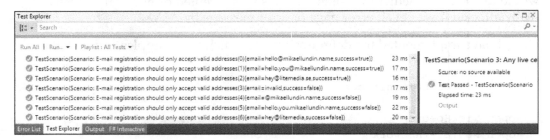

This is the essence of data-driven testing, where we can have the data expressed in a readable format and pushed through our tests without much setup.

Web-browser-based testing

When working with web-based interfaces, the best way to execute functional testing is to query the website and assert on the result HTML. There are some tools and methods to go about doing this, and we will now take a look at a few of them.

Before starting, it is worth discussing where this testing will take place. Before you can use a web client to functionally test a website, you need to deploy this website somewhere. You also need to set up the website with a predictable state so the test doesn't fail because an editor has moved around some content.

How to set up a web-based application is very targeted to the application. Often, you will base a new website on **Content Management System (CMS)**, and this system has its own methods to set up a particular state. Sometimes, however, it is enough to roll back a database backup before the test suite runs, and at other times, you need to create a remote procedure that will set up the necessary state for you. At any rate, predictability is key when it comes to automating functional testing.

When working with long-running flows, such as a shopping cart checkout, it will become necessary for you to create an API that will allow your tests to set the current session. If you're also doing manual testing, this could be a web page where one could add any product and promotion with a click of a button instead of the normal flow. If you don't have a manual tester, a remote procedure call might also be suitable to set the state. This will allow your test to start in the middle of the order checkout without the long setup. Experience tells us that long setups in a web client-base testing environment have a tendency to fail and bring a huge part of your test suite with it.

Just make sure you don't ship your application together with the test harness that allows you to directly manipulate the session, as this would be a huge security concern.

Selenium

Selenium has been the most obvious tool to run web browser-based testing for years. It works by scripting your browser to perform a number of tasks and then queries the Document Object Model (DOM) of the browser window. This can be easily done using F#.

Let's start by including **Selenium WebDriver** into our project:

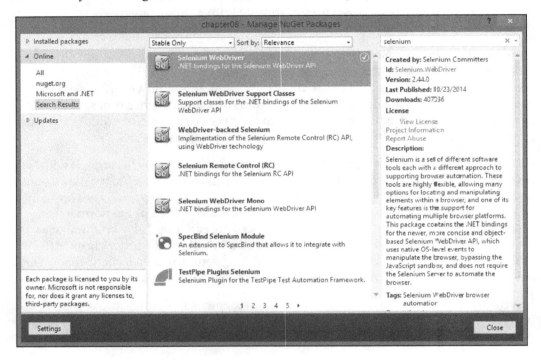

We'll start by writing a simple test that will verify GitHub as the last link in the main navigation on my blog:

```
open OpenQA.Selenium
open OpenQA.Selenium.Chrome
open NUnit.Framework

[<Test>]
let ``my blog should have last link in main navigation to github`` ()
=
    // open browser
    use browser = new ChromeDriver()

    // navigate to page
```

```
browser.Navigate().GoToUrl("http://blog.mikaellundin.name")

// find navigation
let navigation = browser.FindElementByClassName("navigation")

// extract links
let links = navigation.FindElements(By.XPath("//li/a"))

// get last link
let lastLink = links.[links.Count - 1]

// should contain github in address
Assert.That(lastLink.GetAttribute("href"), Contains.
Substring("github"))
```

Here, I am using **ChromeDriver**. In order to get this to work, you need to download
an executable and put it in the current working directory for your test runner. The
executable can be found at `http://chromedriver.storage.googleapis.com/`
`index.html`.

This was very useful, but not very reusable. There should also be a Twitter link in
my main navigation, and in order to test this, I would have to write the same code
all over again. In order to avoid doing so, we can introduce the **Page Object** pattern.

This simply means that a class can represent each page type that we're testing and
the class can have properties, which are things you will find on the page, and also
methods, which represent things you can do on the page, such as logging in.
An example of this is as follows:

```
// represents <a href="">text</a>
type Link = { Href : string; Text : string }

// helper method to create a link from IWebElement
type Link with
    static member Create (element : IWebElement) =
        { Href = element.GetAttribute("href"); Text = element.Text }

// wrapping up list of links into a Navigation type
type Navigation = Link list

// represents the start page
type StartPage (browser : IWebDriver) =
```

```
        let urlPart = "/"
        let baseUrl = ConfigurationManager.AppSettings.["BaseUrl"]

        let navigationClassName = "navigation"
        let navigationLinkXPath = "//li/a"

        // move the browser session to the start page
        member this.NavigateTo () =
            browser.Navigate().GoToUrl(baseUrl + urlPart)

        // the main navigation on the page
        member this.Navigation : Navigation =
            let navigationElement = browser.FindElement(By.
ClassName(navigationClassName))
            let linkElements = navigationElement.FindElements(By.
XPath(navigationLinkXPath))
            [ for linkElement in linkElements ->
Link.Create(linkElement) ]
```

By extracting the details of a page into a type, we can reuse this in other tests running on the same page. When something changes in the HTML structure of that page, we only need to fix it in the type part. The tests that use this type stay the same.

Another great improvement made is related to the readability of the tests:

```
[<Test>]
let ``my blog should have a link to twitter in main navigation`` () =
    // open browser
    use browser = new ChromeDriver()

    // create a start page
    let startPage = new StartPage(browser)

    // navigate to page
    startPage.NavigateTo()

    // find navigation
    let navigation = startPage.Navigation

    // has link to twitter
    let hasLinkToTwitter = navigation |> List.exists (fun link ->
link.Href.Contains("twitter"))

    // assert
    Assert.True(hasLinkToTwitter)
```

The beauty here is that the test doesn't know anything about the internals of the page structure. It only knows what it should expect of the page: that there is a navigation and that navigation contains a link. Then, it asserts that one of those links is indeed directed to Twitter.

As you may have noticed, I didn't output the URL to the page in the code this time around. Instead, I chose to put it in the appSettings file. This is important in order to run the same test on different environments. By changing the appSettings value, I can run the same test suite on my test, stage and production environments without breaking a sweat. Web browser-driven tests are also very useful when websites switch addresses, such as from HTTP to HTTPS.

The problem with web browser-driven tests is that those tests are really slow. Compared to a unit test that should execute in 1 ms, these tests are 5,000 times slower. This quickly becomes a problem because no developer will wait 50 seconds before checking in, as they are likely running 10 web tests at the same time.

I was running a project one time where we had quite a complex payment flow that we covered with web browser-driven tests. We had about 600 tests with a mean execution time of 40 seconds due to the complexity. There were simply a lot of things the browser would have to do before executing the actual test and asserting the result. If you do the math, you end up with between 5 and 6 hours to run the whole test suite, so we did this in the night. When we came back morning after, we received the report indicating whether we had broken something the previous day. This works fine in theory.

There were other things going on at night, however. There was a complete database backup job, that would make the whole site unresponsive for 20 minutes. This would cause a random set of tests to fail every night, and we would never know which ones. Once we got around this problem, we still had random false positives in the test run because of conflicts with night-based jobs.

The end result was that the test suite was green for 2 days out of the whole year. The effect this has on a team is that they simply don't look at the test report because it's always red. A red test run, at least in this case, however, doesn't mean the functionality is broken; it just means the test wasn't a success.

All this came from having very slow tests at a very large scale. Web-browser-based testing is hard to run in parallel because of session cookies. Once you start going down the path of optimizing your web browser-based tests, you will spend more time than it took to write them.

The following sections will propose what we can do about this.

PhantomJS

PhantomJS is a headless web browser, meaning it doesn't present pages in a graphical manner. Instead, it provides an API which you can use to control the browser and query its contents.

This is really useful for functional testing purposes. With this, you can easily test your web frontends without the need of opening a browser window. The browser window is a major side effect of your tests that can cause all kinds of trouble:

- The test suite needs to interact with the desktop, which is not always appropriate, for example, when you're running your tests on a build server. There are solutions for this, though.

- The test can fail at any given time because something else grabbed the focus of the browser window.

- The test can fail because something is trying to interact with the browser window, such as an installed add-on.

These are some of the headaches of browser testing, along with trusted zones and certificate errors. Some of these can be avoided by running a headless browser, such as PhantomJS, instead. This browser is based on **WebKit**, and so is closest to Safari and Chrome in its implementation.

Of course, this does not apply if what you're testing is cross-browser compatibility.

To enable this, we can use Selenium, which we're already familiar with. Before you can do this, you need to download the Windows package of PhantomJS from `http://phantomjs.org/`, or just download it using the **NuGet Package Manager**:

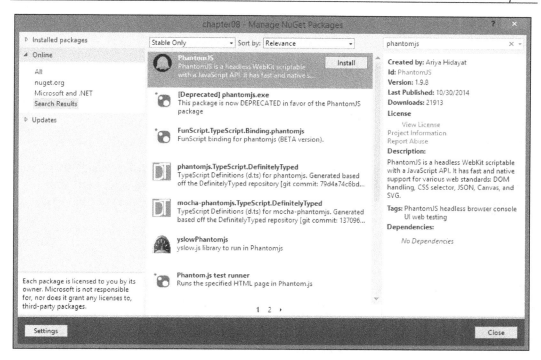

Now, we can write a simple test like this to make sure it works:

```
open OpenQA.Selenium
open OpenQA.Selenium.Internal
open OpenQA.Selenium.PhantomJS
open NUnit.Framework
open FsUnit

[<Test>]
let ``homepage should have 'Mikael Lundin' in the title`` () =
    // arrange
```

```
use browser = new PhantomJSDriver()

// act
browser.Navigate().GoToUrl("http://mikaellundin.name')

// assert
browser.Title |> should contain "Mikael Lundin"
```

The rest consists of just following the standard Selenium implementation practices.

Sadly, it is still slow, so it doesn't remove all the pains of web browser-based testing; however, it does help with some of the more practical problems listed earlier. If we really need to reduce the time it takes to execute the test suite, we need to step away from the web browser for a while and look at our alternatives.

Canopy

There is an F# framework called Canopy that provides a frictionless functional layer on top of Selenium. The goal of this web testing framework is to provide a stable API that is quick to learn and is clean and concise.

Canopy tests run in a console application. Most testing frameworks have their tests built in a library, but with Canopy, you can build and execute your tests as an executable.

Make sure that in the properties of your test project, the framework version is > 4.0, and the output type is the console application:

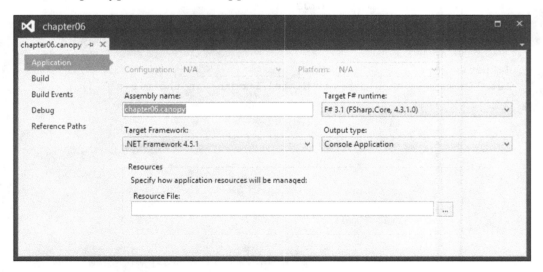

All you have to do to get started is include Canopy in your testing project from the
NuGet Package Manager window:

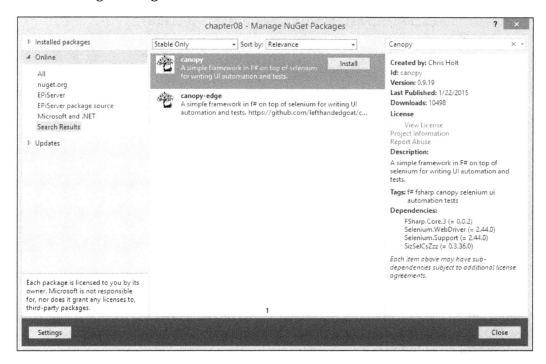

Now, you can begin to write your first test:

```
open canopy
open runner
open System

[<EntryPoint>]
let main argv =

    //start an instance of the firefox browser
    start firefox

    // grouping for tests
    context "Blog start page"

    // define a test
    "blog title should contain Mikael Lundin" &&& fun _ ->
        // navigate
```

```
        url "http://blog.mikaellundin.name"

        // assert
        contains "MIKAEL LUNDIN" (read "#blog-title")

    // define a test
    "number of post excerpts should be 5" &&& fun _ ->
        // navigate
        url "http://blog.mikaellundin.name"

        // assert
        count ".post-excerpt" 5

//run all tests
run()

// close browser window
quit()

// return an integer exit code
0
```

When running the executable, it will open a web browser, execute the tests, and then close the browser upon executing the `quit()` function. The output in the console window will be as follows:

```
context: Blog start page
Test: blog title should contain Mikael Lundin
Passed
Test: number of post excerpts should be 5
Passed

0 minutes 1 seconds to execute
2 passed
0 failed
```

The syntax that Canopy brings to web testing matches functional programming very neatly, but it does simplify the problem a bit too much and doesn't provide an API to support more advanced assertions that you would be able to perform with direct access to Selenium. Canopy may lower the bar for writing tests, but depending on what's being tested, using Selenium directly might be a better choice.

For full reference of Canopy, please visit its project page on GitHub at
`http://lefthandedgoat.github.io/canopy/`.

CSQuery

In order to speed things up, the only option we have is to simplify the process, and
we can do this by cutting out the web browser from the equation, as it is simply
too slow.

In some cases where we want to test content and not interact, a browser is just in the
way and we could settle with an `HttpClient` class. The messy part comes when you
try to assert on the result, and this is where CSQuery comes into the picture.

CSQuery is a port of jQuery to C#, but of course, it's usable in all .NET languages.
We can use it to run assertions on the DOM tree of the page we've downloaded with
the `HttpClient` class.

Let's start by including CSQuery into our project:

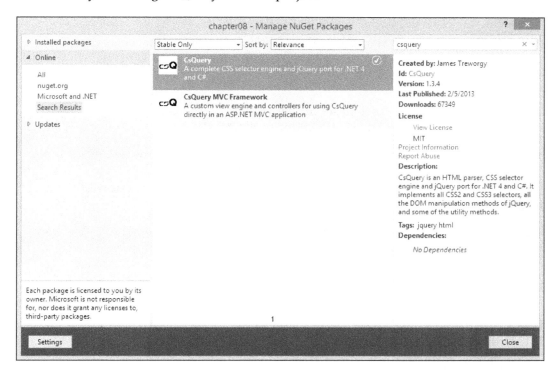

Now, we can write a test that will download a page from a URL and assert on the page's information:

```
open System.Net
open CsQuery
open NUnit.Framework
open FsUnit

[<Test>]
let ``there should be at least 5 blog posts pushed from start page``
() =
    // open new web client
    use client = new WebClient()

    // download the html we're testing
    let html = client.DownloadString("http://blog.mikaellundin.name")

    // parse the DOM
    let dom = CQ(html)

    // query the DOM for the blog posts
    let posts = dom.[".post-excerpt"]

    // assert that number of posts > 4
    posts.Length |> should be (greaterThan 4)
```

This code does not offer much more ceremony than Selenium. We're using standard .NET functionality to get the HTML, and then we use CSQuery to parse the HTML.

This test runs in 500 ms, which makes it one-sixth of what the browser tests would take; however, it is still very slow because of the network traffic. If you're able to run your testing target locally and test against it, I'm sure you could get down to tens of milliseconds without a blink.

This is clearly very unsuitable for any scenario in which you interact with the web page and want to test that interaction. Let's say you log in and perform a number of tasks as an authenticated user; this is something you wouldn't want to use CSQuery for.

Another obvious thing is that scripts are not run on the page. If your tests rely on JavaScript, then CSQuery is completely useless to you. This will just download the HTML as is and assert on it.

The perfect scenario for CSQuery is when you want to test that the content has rendered correctly on the page. This is where you don't need a full-fledged browser to render the page, but could be satisfied with querying the resultant HTML.

Regression testing

Any test that doesn't bring value is a waste and should be deleted, because it still comes with the cost of maintenance. The hard part is to discover which tests are valueless and which are invaluable.

As a software tester, it is easy to draw the conclusion that every test provides regression, where regression means that it validates no new bugs appear in the functionality we covered with tests. This might be true in some cases, but it is wrong to make this assumption when it wasn't the purpose of the test. Unit and integration testing may provide some regression testing, but this comes as a side effect and not as its primary focus. In unit testing, the purpose is design, and in integration testing, the purpose is to validate how parts of the system fit together. These purposes have very little to do with regression.

When it comes to functional testing, regression is another matter. In a functional test, I claim to expect some functionality of the system from a black box perspective. We do not care how the system comes to the expected output, only that it does. When the implementation of the system changes, the unit tests will need to be refactored and the integration tests will fail, but the functional test will stay the same as long as the system stays true to its purpose. In this sense, it is a perfect regression test. Stating what we know to be true about a system is the only regression test that can be trusted.

The most common reason why the existing functionality stops working is that there is a change or fix made to the code that has a side effect the author didn't think about. Most often with these fixes, its not the original author of the code that does the fix. As such, this new developer might not understand the functionality completely, and in this regard, he or she fails to fulfill all its requirements. This is why there are regression tests in place, in order to ensure what we know about the function remains true after the change.

A good practice when dealing with changes in an existing code base is to start by expressing that change in a test that will turn up red until the change is implemented. This way, you're not only covered on old functionality, but also on any subsequent changes. This gives you a good regression test suite, as you only test on requirements that have been requested by the product owner and not on things you might believe will break, because this is often untrue. Before checking out the next chapter, there is a more advanced topic on test automation found online, *Chapter 11, Property-Based Testing*. If you thirst for more functional testing code, I suggest you head there before continuing with the rest of the book.

Summary

In the end, we want to have a fully featured test suite that describes how the system works. This specification will be the best documentation available for your system, as it will get verified every time a developer commits code to the solution. It will provide a layer of protection indicating that the functionality stays the same throughout the application life cycle.

The main challenge with functional testing will always be to create a test suite that runs fast enough and provides predictable results so we can trust the process. Functional tests are the hardest to write in plenty, and they still make a fast-running and stable test suite. We need to manage this in order to stay sane and keep providing value.

7
The Controversy of Test Automation

Testing is hard. It is hard to find the right balance in testing to know what to test and what to skip. It is also hard to write high-quality tests that bring more value than the effort it took to produce them.

However, the value of a good test suite is tremendous and shouldn't be neglected by fear of learning or challenging what is difficult. This chapter will focus on the difficulties and teach you how to think about testing and quality measures in general.

In this chapter, we will cover the following topics:

- Bugs or defects
- The cost of quality
- The false security of code coverage
- Test-driven development
- Testing or fact-checking

After this chapter, you will feel confident about applying test automation to your project. This will help you to not only decide when to write a test and when to sustain, but also to know how to test. This chapter is a fast track in the experiences of test automation and quality in software development.

Bugs or defects

There are some glossary terms for software testers regarding how they should label the result of their testing, namely error, fault, bug, or failure. These do not completely apply to test automation. As the terms fault and bug are interchangeable, I would consider the list antiquated.

As programmers, we see the code from an inside-out perspective and do not think of familiarizing ourselves with software testers' terms. This is also why we have one common name for a fault, and that is bug. The problem with this term appears when clients find a bug and you as a developer insist it's the intended behavior.

It is a common misconception that code can only be right or wrong. In reality, however, there are many gray zones of software failure that can cause real trouble.

The following image is a map around quality in a software project:

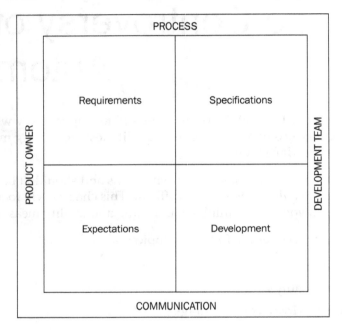

A software failure can come from missing or vague requirements. It can also come from weak specifications that don't make it clear what to expect of the features developed. It is common that the expectation of the product owner is different from the team that is actually developing the feature. Then, there is development done by developers that sometimes has human errors, for example, typos.

The quality of a product is a contract between the product owner and the development team, and what holds it all together is process and communication.

Bugs

Let's say the tester on your team comes to you and says, "I expected to get an updated total price when I put the products in the shopping cart." If this report comes as a surprise because you thought you'd written it that way, then it's a bug.

Bugs can be described as a scenario in which the code was intended to do X, but instead does Y. This means that the developer has made a mistake and this has resulted in a bug. Both the tester and developer agree that there is a fault in the software.

The following are examples of bugs in a web application:

- Clicking on the **Submit** button should submit the form, but it doesn't seem to do anything
- No confirmation e-mail is sent out at the end of the order process
- After increasing the quantity of line items in the shopping cart, the quantity number resets to the previous number after the page is reloaded

The strangest observations I've made about bugs are the ability for them to reappear. A bug is fixed and the solution is deployed to production. The client confirms that the bug is fixed and the issue is closed in the bug-tracking software. However, after the next deployment, the bug is back and no one can explain how it happened.

How to avoid them

No programmer is perfect; even we often fail to recognize bugs in software projects. Instead, we have a healthy number of errors produced for every thousand lines of code. There are several reasons for this:

- The programmer is human and can make errors
- The feature is rushed because of the project plan
- The work environment contains distractions
- The requirements or specification is misunderstood
- The developer is not well-versed in the technologies used

I have yet to meet a programmer that doesn't produce bugs.

A while back, I was working with a client who had very little IT project experience. The project was running late because of a high number of bugs that were found during the user acceptance test. The client came up with the following suggestion:

Why not do it right the first time?

The project manager guffawed over the client's ignorance and went into a rampage on how it was impossible to work with these inexperienced product owners. My answer to the project owner was as follows:

The client is right. We should do it right the first time, but that would require a higher initial investment in quality.

The project manager walked away.

The writing of this book is a similar scenario. I have a tool that checks spelling and grammar so I can correct them before sending the text to my editor, who will then proofread and give suggestions on how to change the content in order to better meet the requirements of my readers.

All code should be considered a draft until it has been through the quality assurance process the team has previously decided upon.

The following table describes different quality measures that can be used to validate code:

Quality measure	Description
Statically typed language	Prevents lexical and semantic errors by compiling the code
Static code analysis	Prevents logical errors by parsing the code to match the rules
Test automation	Prevents logical errors by verifying the code and writing consuming code
Code review	Prevents logical errors by having another developer review the code
System testing	Verifies that the product fulfills the requirements

There will always be errors in the code we write. As software developers, we have to accept that we're the source of errors in our software and we need to do what we can to mitigate this.

The only way to avoid bugs from coming back is to use the method of writing tests that verifies the bug is fixed and makes sure the test will run for every subsequent commit. Then, you don't have to deal with the embarrassment of explaining to the client why a bug has reappeared after being fixed and needs to be fixed again.

Defects

Imagine a feature has been released for a user acceptance test. It has been implemented according to the specification and fulfills the requirements. Still, the client comes back saying, "This is not as I expected." This means the feature has a defect.

A defect can be described as the state in which the developer intended the code to do X and the code does X, but the client was expecting Y.

The client will call it a bug, but the developer will claim that the code does as intended. The project manager will then come in and call it a change in order to charge the client for it.

The following are examples of defects in a web application:

- The client expected to be redirected back to the start page after a successful shopping cart checkout
- The client expected they wouldn't be able to put more products into the shopping cart than there is in the inventory
- The client expected that clicking the logo of the web page would take them back to the start page

The problem is in the way that features are communicated. It's caused by a faulty alignment between expectations of the client and the implementation of the developer. This might not be considered a code problem, but it is a huge problem for software as it represents the first line of changes to the code that will cause it to be more complex.

How to avoid them

The only way to avoid defects is to ensure the team and client are working in close collaboration, both in planning and on a day-to-day basis. The client should be included in daily standups and approving the feature specifications so there are no surprises coming out of development.

The following points explain how to avoid defects:

- Create detailed specifications
- Have the product owner and tester review the specifications
- Ensure the client and team are working in close collaboration to align expectations

Fewer defects will lead to fewer changes, which will lead to higher quality of the code. This quality will lead to fewer bugs. Communication is an all upward spiral of quality.

The difference between bugs and defects

In order to avoid bugs, we need to improve the coding process, and we can do this with a variety of tools that will verify the programmer hasn't committed any faults.

In order to avoid defects, we need to improve the process and communication between the development team and product owner to ensure that they are aligned with regard to requirements and specifications.

The cost of quality

Bugs are the major unpredictable factor in software development projects. It's what makes projects run late. Wouldn't it be great if we could write bug- and defect-free software? Imagine a project where no testers are needed because no bugs are created. Is this even possible? Is it something to strive for?

We are a young and immature industry. This is obvious from how many projects are running late, over budget, or simply canceled. We try to run our projects as if we're building bridges, and we like to compare our industry professionals to surgeons.

Our bridges, they fall, but we can't blame the materials or force majeure. We can only blame ourselves and our own ignorance, and vow that next time, we will focus more on quality and build a better bridge.

Quality index

The software development quality index is the number of bugs and defects produced for each **Thousands of Lines of Code (KLOC)**.

The following image describes the software development quality index:

$$\frac{bugs}{kLOC} = qualityindex$$

The quality index should be as low as possible. It is a relative indicator of the quality of the solution, and It is best measured over time in order to make decisions regarding quality measures.

The following image shows how the quality index can be measured in a Scrum project:

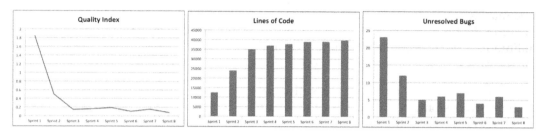

The quality index is directly proportional to the amount of code and bugs in that code. If you measure these things by each sprint, you can visualize the quality of the software in a simple line chart.

If the quality index is decreasing, it means there are fewer unresolved bugs for each KLOC. This could mean that the quality of the product is increasing, or it could mean that the quality of testing is decreasing. This is difficult to determine, but a decreasing quality index is preferred.

If the quality index is increasing, it means there are more unresolved bugs for each KLOC in the product. This could mean that the quality of the product is decreasing. It could also mean that the quality of testing is increasing.

The quality index is directly affected by the ability of the team to solve bugs. If the team doesn't have time to solve bugs during the sprint, the quality index will increase and the technical debt will build up.

The quality index is a black box measurement. It doesn't take code quality or practices into account. If there are no bugs in the software, it is of high-quality. If the team is able to manage a product with bad code and practices and still keep the number of bugs down, the quality index will be low and the product will be presumed to have high-quality.

The software craftsman

Software craftsmanship is a movement that compares developers with carpenters. You start out as an apprentice learning the craft, become intermediate after delivering some successful or failed projects, and eventually end up being a master.

The master software craftsman is always up to date with the latest technologies, pushing the boundaries of his or her team and the solutions produced. He or she maintains a weblog, attends conferences, and runs a few open source projects in the evenings.

These craftsmen have a disease. This disease makes them strive for quality because of their professional conduct. They don't want to be seen delivering software that is not in its prime condition, so they strive for quality for quality's sake.

Instead of seeing the value of the features, they focus on the value of the code. They spend hours setting up continuous integration, **Test-driven Development (TDD)**, automation, and processes. These things do not deliver value to the client, unless it helps in getting features deployed to production. This is shown in the following image:

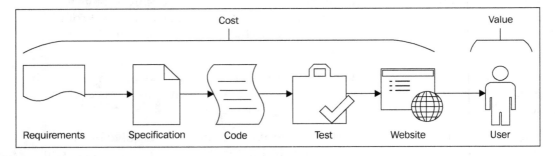

Features start out as requirements and these requirements are elaborated into specifications. The specifications turn into code and the code turns into a test. Tests turn into a pre-production environment and then turns into a live feature. This is when users first reap the benefits of the feature, as it generates value. Every step before the user is a cost, which should be considered waste if no one is using the feature.

Long before thinking of quality, one should consider the following:

- How much value does the feature bring?
- How many users will the feature have?
- How long do we expect the feature to exist?

Then, we can start discussing how large of a quality effort is needed to bring the most out of the feature.

Not all code is created equal

Not all developers want to create the perfect solution to the perfect problem. Most actually just want to do a good job, meet their deadlines, and go home in the evening to their families. The software craftsman finds it a waste of time to not spend the evening on research or open source projects. There is, however, something admirable and predictable about the 9–5 programmer.

The success of a software project is about creating predictability, and this is not only done by processes, but also by composing a team of predictable people. Not everyone in the team will be a rock star, but every team member should bring predictable results. Knowing your team and stocking it with the right people is the path to success.

All programmers have their own tools and skillset. They will attack a problem based on their own experiences. This makes code we write very diverse. And there is not one solution to any given problem, not even a better solution. There are as many solutions as there are programmers. This will all lead to some diversity in the quality produced by the team members.

Some developers write their tests first and others do this at the end. Many developers might not want to write tests at all. It is a challenge to find common ground and select the practices that may be done based on individual preferences and those that must be enforced.

Being a pragmatic programmer

A duct tape programmer is one that rolls up the sleeves and gets down to business no matter how ugly the situation might be. This type of practice is the opposite of finding a generalized solution to the type of problem you want to solve. Instead, you look at what's asked for and use the bare minimum to make it work.

I was once paired with a C# developer, writing a self-help service for the client's website where they could log in, look at their issues, and track progress. He needed a way of parsing out e-mail addresses from an input string and wanted my help. I had already been doing this same thing for the backend service, so I simply told him to copy my code into his solution.

However, the developer said, "This is not **Don't Repeat Yourself** (**DRY**). Should we reuse what you did in the backend?" I said, "Yes, we're doing that by copying my code." It meant we had to maintain the code in two places, but that could be done at a lower cost compared to implementing a SOAP web service in order to expose the regular expression for the e-mail.

We ended up copying the code, violating DRY for the greater good.

The value of the code is in the feature being used. This value decreases when there is an extensive amount of maintenance needed to be done on that code. This is the risk of duct tape solutions. If it breaks, you'll spend an unreasonable amount of time fixing it. Still, the generalized solution often requires time in creation, and it still doesn't promise to save you time on maintenance.

Good enough

Bugs cost money. They also cost time that could be better spent working on a new functionality. They are responsible for pushing deadlines, and they cause the downtime of your site. A bug is associated with not just annoyance, but cost.

If you can put a price on a bug, you can also decide how much money you're willing to spend in order to avoid one.

Before starting a software development project, I usually ask the client what they wish to prioritize out of the following attributes:

- Cost efficiency
- High-quality
- Many features

It gives a good direction for the team to go in when planning and specifying features. If the client answers that they want all 3 in a healthy mix, you know you're in trouble.

I had this rare client that put quality above all. Nothing else mattered, and we could spend as many hours as we'd like as long as it provided a qualitative solution.

I didn't want to challenge the client on this, but still I asked why this was the case, and the client made this argument: We have 5,000 orders from the website any given Monday. Each order is worth 50€. This is an income of 2,50,000€ every day; when divided throughout the day, it becomes roughly 10,500€ an hour. We hire you for 100 € an hour, which means you could spend 105 hours on quality if it were to give the website 1 more hour of uptime.

Needless to say, the requirement was 99.995 percent uptime, which meant they allowed 25 minute planned maintenance every year.

There are many different quality improvements that can be applied to a code base or development process. Each will cost a little and improve on the quality index. As a development team, it is important to pick the low-hanging fruit first, so to speak, in order to reap big benefits with little effort.

More quality improvements will eventually lead to less benefits, and there is a time when a team should stop working on improving the quality and focus on delivering the feature.

The following image shows how the value of quality measures decreases:

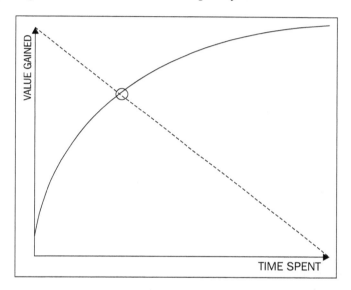

At the dotted line, the amount of effort spent is equal to the value gained. Spending any more time in testing would be a waste.

An experienced developer will know where the spending of quality improvements matches the cost of the bugs and where the cost of quality improvement exceeds the value returned.

In a project I was running as a Scrum Master, we always took the opportunity at the start of the sprint demo to review how many bugs were created and solved them during the sprint. The following graph is from this very project:

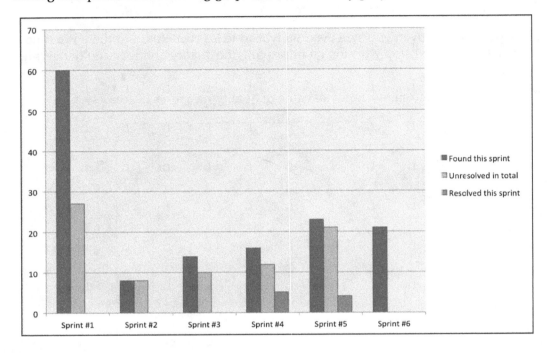

With these metrics, you can easily determine how much time was spent on fixing bugs and come up with a number regarding how much these bugs cost the development project with each sprint. This would give you a good estimate on how much effort should be spent in order to avoid these bugs.

Technical debt

Writing code is never easy, and it doesn't get easier when you have external dependencies in the process, such as deadlines. The project manager will likely ask you to cut some corners in order to deliver the feature to the client as per the deadline. This will make you skip some of the quality processes, such as tests and peer review, in order to deliver faster.

The result might be delivered faster, but with lower quality and some built-up technical debt.

The debt you owe to quality will cost the project interest for every feature added. This will make the features more expensive and make bugs appear more easily. This will be the case until the debt is repaid. Repaying a debt is done by refactoring the code and adding the quality measures that were skipped in order to deliver faster. Doing so will be much more expensive after the feature has already been delivered, and this is the price that has to be paid for cutting corners.

Technical debt is not at all bad. It will enable you to make a choice. Is it worth cutting corners on quality in order to meet a deadline? Sometimes the cost of fixing the code after the deadline is worth the debt. In that case, one should opt for the debt, but not forget to pay it off. This is where many software projects fail.

The false security of code coverage

When doing test automation, you can use a tool that will tell you how large a part of your code is covered by tests. This may seem like a good idea at first glance, but does have some hidden dangers.

The following image shows the code coverage tool, **NCover**:

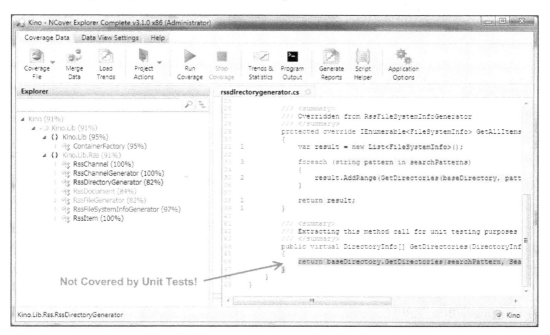

The code coverage report will show you what code was traversed and how many times, but it's a false assumption that the report will tell you what was tested. How many times is it required that a test pass a line of code in order to call it covered? Consider the following example:

```
open NUnit.Framework
open FsUnit

// System Under Test
let rec fibonacci = function
    | n when n < 2 -> 1
    | n -> fibonacci (n - 2) + fibonacci (n - 1)

let fibonacciSeq x = [0..(x - 1)] |> List.map fibonacci

[<Test>]
let returns_correct_result () =
    fibonacciSeq 5 |> should equal [1; 1; 2; 3; 5]
```

The test is written only to traverse all the code in one go. It doesn't have a clear purpose of what it is trying to test, and it doesn't specify what is expected of the functionality:

```
[<Test>]
let ``should expect 1 to be the first fibonnaci number`` () =
    fibonacci 0 |> should equal 1

[<Test>]
let ``should expect 1 to be the second fibonnaci number`` () =
    fibonacci 1 |> should equal 1

[<Test>]
let ``should expect 5 to be the fifth fibonnaci number`` () =
    fibonacci 4 |> should equal 5

[<Test>]
let ``should expect 1, 1, 2, 3, 5 to be the five first fibonnaci
numbers`` () =
    fibonacciSeq 5 |> should equal [1; 1; 2; 3; 5]
```

A function will be fully covered very rarely because there are too many execution paths to follow, and it's difficult to follow each and every one of them. The test coverage report will give the developer a false sense of security, and it has an even worse effect in the hands of an ignorant project manager. Test coverage should be considered more harmful than useful.

The one and only benefit of test coverage reports is to analyze where testing has been left out and where to focus testing efforts. However, if such a report is needed, there should be a change in how software development is done to have a more proactive take on quality assurance, instead of building technical debt and analyzing where the issues are in retrospect.

Measuring the delta of code coverage

The natural next step in code coverage is to create a report that will measure how coverage changes from one version of the code to another. There is software that can help you produce such reports in the build server, as shown in the following graph:

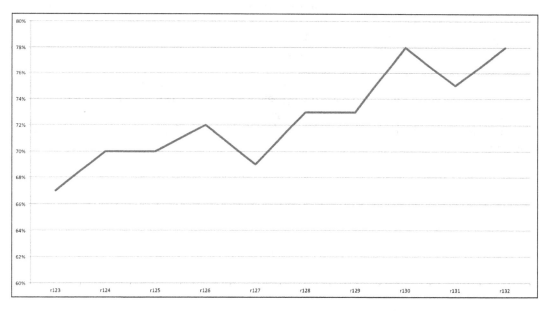

The problem with such a report is that it will be used as a measurement of quality, where it is no such thing. It might provide insights into rising technical debt, but without a trained eye and knowledge of the code that has been committed, the report might cause more harm than good.

There have been talks of development teams that have a requirement to never let coverage percentage (%) decrease. If they commit code that has lower coverage percentage than the previous commit, the build fails until it has been covered by tests.

These is the sort of quality measures that are disruptive to the software development process and cause development to progress much slower. It will not cause quality to rise substantially because programmers will write tests that cover as much code as possible so the build will not fail.

Skip the code coverage tools and reports and put your trust in your methods and processes instead.

Test-driven development

In the beginning there were these brilliant Java guys who wondered what would happen if you were to write code that executed some other piece of code in order to verify whether the original code worked. They created a framework called JUnit that was designed to help others write code to test other code. This idea got very popular and has since forked into many different frameworks on different platforms.

The guys behind this idea were Erich Gamma and Kent Beck, and thought of as leaders, they didn't stop at discovering test automation, but instead asked themselves, "What would happen if we write the **test first** and the system later?" This invention was labeled TDD and has since been the subject of countless discussions and controversy.

The workflow they invented is shown in the following image:

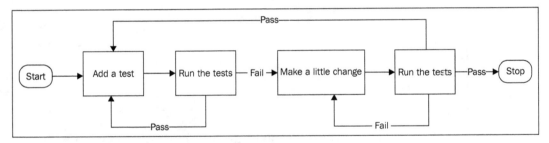

The workflow illustrates writing the test first. If the test passes, the system under test already has this functionality implemented. If the test fails, the functionality needs to be implemented into the system. The system should be finalized until all the tests pass. Once they do, the developer may continue by implementing the next test; otherwise, he or she is done implementing the feature.

The point of developing software using the test first approach is that you drive the design of the system from the tests, forcing the system to produce a public API where the tests can hook in to verify. You work in increments in which the system has gradually created unit for unit, where you only implement enough to satisfy the test of the current unit, keeping the design simplistic and non-generalized.

The benefits of TDD is that the developer is forced to stop thinking about what his or her code will output before he or she starts writing it. Instead of having a solution coming from the mind directly to implementation, there is a middle step- the thought process we call design, which is formalized in a test before the implementation of the actual feature. This leads to cleaner code, but also code that is better anchored in the requirements.

Red, green, refactor

It quickly became obvious with TDD that it was hard to maintain a larger perspective of the architecture when working outward with the system, unit for unit. Instead, the systems developed in this way quickly became an entanglement of units, which were all very well designed, but together created a complex graph of dependency. From these problems, the red, green, refactor model was born.

The following image shows the red, green, refactor model:

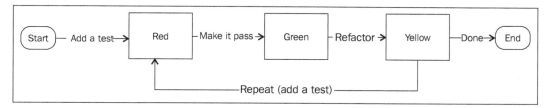

First, the developer writes a test that will not pass and therefore will be red. Then, the system is implemented in the most trivial way so the test turns green. After the test turns green, the developer moves on to refactoring the code, making sure it fits the rest of the system and the rest of the system fits it. Once refactoring is complete, the developer is either done or continues by implementing the next test to complete the feature.

It is important that the test is red once written. If the test turns green immediately, it indicates that too much has been implemented to make another test green. The effect is that you skip the refactoring step when tests turn green as soon as they are written.

Refactoring is the missing piece of the TDD puzzle, and also the most important one. It is the art of taking a piece of code and improving its design without changing its function. By doing this, the developer will get around the side effects that were associated with TDD in the beginning and get large test-driven systems with good design.

The difficulty, and at the same time, benefit, of TDD is that the developer needs to know beforehand how the feature will be implemented. There is not much room for trial and error, as it is a common practice of developers.

Aversions to test-driven development

A couple of years ago, TDD was very hyped up and strongly evangelized by thought leaders in the software development industry. One of these individuals was Uncle Bob (Robert C. Martin), a strong spokesperson in the .NET community who claimed that 100 percent coverage was the only way to perform TDD.

We have since grown up as an industry and discovered that 100 percent coverage is a waste, as it encourages developers to write terrible tests just to reach the end goal.

The arguments that have sprung up against TDD in the last few years are as follows:

- Project managers mandate developers to perform 100 percent test coverage, which encourages them to write terrible tests just to meet the goal.

- Not all code provide much value in being tested, such as wrappers, facades, or build scripts.

- The test suite also needs development and maintenance. In order to bring more value than cost to a project, it needs to be managed.

- Some tests are better performed manually, when it's easy for a human to check whether the result is plausible, but difficult for a computer.

Your system bloats because of all the code that is needed in order to support your test. There are many test doubles and test interfaces necessary in order to properly call the system under test. This code also needs maintenance and refactoring as the code base grows, and it has the risk of becoming a framework of itself, as well.

A good example of TDD not working is best understood while working with **Cascading Style Sheets (CSS)**. Every rule in CSS is directly connected to a graphical representation on the screen. There is no good way of verifying that the rendering is correct, using test automation.

How do you test CSS first? The nature of working with CSS is that you write a rule, see what happens on the screen, and then adjust until the result matches the design.

It is not sensible to try writing tests first for this layer. The only way to get it right is to use a human to check whether the result looks accurate.

The test-driven development movement started out as a mind hack in order to write software in a different way. Many feel that fundamentalists have taken over with a louder and angrier rhetoric, making other developers feel bad for not testing or not writing tests first. It might have been necessary, however, to beat down the nonbelievers and declare them unprofessional to cause developers to start writing tests. Ultimately, it has divided the developer community into testers and non-testers.

Test first development

At the time when TDD first became all the rage and a source of great frustration and controversy, it became hard to label work that was being done as TDD without implying that tests were written before the code, as in the **Beck/Gamma** model.

However, most developers that were writing tests were not doing it in a test first manner, but called themselves TDD practitioners anyway. The only way to keep the concepts apart was to start calling it test first and test-last, where the purists claimed the only way of doing it right is to write tests first, and that **test-last** really has nothing to do with test-driven development.

Pragmatists will always claim that writing tests last has greater value than not writing tests at all, in situations where tests bring more value to the development process than writing the code without.

Many developers have a hard time adjusting to the reversed thought process of testing first that requires you to visualize a fair amount inside your mind before you start writing the first test.

 Don't feel bad for not writing tests first. The purpose is not the process, but the result.

Fixing bugs

The test first approach lends itself very well to fixing bugs in your code. You take advantage of tests being specifications and use this to both verify the bug is there and that it is fixed. This will provide regression, making sure the bug will not reappear.

The following image shows the workflow for fixing bug tests first:

The first thing you need to do is add a test to fill the gap provided by the bug. The test should turn red; otherwise, you have not managed to find the bug. After this, you can fix the bug, which will cause the test to turn green and give you an instant verification that the bug is fixed.

Don't forget to refactor the code if needed.

Using this workflow extensively for bugs, I've discovered a few things:

1. It is quite common for you to find out that the system actually works as expected, but that the bug report was wrong.

2. It is also common that you fix a bug, but the test doesn't turn green because you only thought you'd fixed it, when it's actually still there.

3. It is common that you fix the bug only to discover another test turns red. Your fix broke something else that now needs fixing.

4. It sometimes happens that you fix a bug and now another test has turned red, which contradicts the first test. The reported bug was a change of requirements in disguise.

All these things that get unraveled by fixing bug tests first means I will save time for both myself and the tester by iterating fewer times.

API design

Another situation where the test first approach really excels is in **Application Program Interface (API)** design. By specifying the API by the tests you write, you're actually the first consumer of that API. This will not only create a well-designed API, but also serve as a good example of how the API can be used.

Here's an example of how tests can specify a search API:

```
open NUnit.Framework

[<Test>]
let ``Search should not accept empty search string`` () =
    Assert.Fail()

[<Test>]
let ``Search should return first page as default`` () =
    Assert.Fail()

[<Test>]
let ``Search should return 20 items per page as default`` () =
    Assert.Fail()

[<Test>]
let ``Search should return all items on 1 page when page size is
zero`` () =
    Assert.Fail()
```

I was once working for a client for whom we had created a very nice type ahead for addresses, namely all addresses in Sweden. The client, who had previously been very skeptic about our solution, was overly thrilled to see it in action and wanted it implemented on all their platforms. One of these was a **WinForms** application maintained by a competitor of ours. This is a classic problem where two vendors competing with each other are forced to collaborate. If anything were to go bad, there would be a lot of blaming, which would not help the client gain anything at all.

In order to keep concerns separated, I was assigned with implementing the API that would service the competitor with the search functionality that was featured in the type ahead.

I started out by gathering the requirements, working out what tests I needed to confirm that the search API was working. I implemented each test one at a time until I had a completely green test suite. I shipped the API documentation together with the tests so our competitor could run the tests and see that it worked. In a situation where one party is very likely to blame the other for any miscommunication, this method actually worked wonders.

Test-driven development is not a matter of principle or doing things the right way. The only right way is to produce as much value as possible with the least amount of cost. Sometimes, this can mean writing tests first and other times, by writing them after the code. In rare cases, it means writing no tests at all. The important part is to recognize what brings value and implement it.

Testing or fact-checking

Upon asking James Bach, one of the most influential people in software testing, what it means to test, you will receive the answer that it means questioning the given product by operating and observing it. This enables you to make informed decisions about the product.

This definition of testing is quite far away from what we've been talking about so far, and this is because James Bach is talking about manual testing. The process of manual testing is a creative process in which you study and research, resulting in advice and reports to drive a decision. This doesn't sound very much like automation.

What we've been talking about so far is to use tests to drive the design of our code and also as specification for the product. This is a very proactive approach where we let testing drive the innovation of the product itself in comparison to manual testing, which is a reaction to the product that has been created.

The reasons for using automated tests are as follows:

- Test automation is performed at the same time as developing the code, whereas manual testing is done after the feature has been developed.

- These automated tests are written by a developer and not a tester, making it a development task and not a testing task.

- The automated tests will return a binary result determining if they pass or not each time code is committed. This result is different from the test report created by a tester.

- The automated tests are written to avoid creating bugs and producing a system with higher quality. The manual tests are performed to find problems with the product in order to iterate and improve it.

There have been discussions in the developer community if what we do can actually be called testing or whether it should it be called something else.

A few years back there was an initiative to rename automated tests as "examples", but it never really caught on. It is not bad to see test automation as an example of how the system works. However, it doesn't fit into the red, green, refactor method.

Going back to James Bach, he prefers to call it software checking, as what we do will only verify facts that are known about the product. Developers that are really into **Behavior-driven Design (BDD)** are keen on calling tests executable specifications, which is great for a narrow field of the tests that are written.

Even if it doesn't feel quite right, "testing" is the term we're stuck with.

Replacing the tester with automation

It has been a common misunderstanding of the businesses for which I've been consulting that test automation will be able to replace the need of a tester. They seem to think it's a good thing to automate testing so there is no need to hire a tester. From what we've been discussing thus far, this is of course nonsensical as test automation and manual testing are so different, with completely different outcomes and purposes. Test automation will produce a product with fewer bugs, and manual testing will come up with improvement to the product to better solve the problem at hand.

There are situations in which manual testing can reap the benefits of test automation:

- Regression testing, making sure that everything that worked in the previous version is still working, is one area where automation excels. This is also an area where computers are particularly good and where the tester's time is better spent elsewhere.

  There are excellent tools that let the tester automate the checking by recording the test and setting a condition on the result. This will reduce the time spent on regression testing and essentially let the tester spend more time focusing on exploratory testing.

- Humans are particularly bad at coming up with good test data. Computers are lousy at determining good test cases, but quite good at generating random test data. When you want to test something with a lot of diverse data, it is good to use a computer to generate that data in order to achieve unpredictability.

Seeing the many job openings for test automation engineers, I'm not quite sure what they do. They are not hired as developers, so they will not write tests as a part of their development process. They are not hired as testers, so their purpose is not to investigate and question the product. It will be interesting to see the progression of test automation in the future.

Summary

Test automation is still something that is new to the software industry. It is a game changer in terms of quality and making software projects predictable. It is a mind-bending practice that is hard for the uninitiated, but is a valuable tool once learned. It does not replace the tester in your team, and it cannot be used to measure developers' productivity.

In this chapter, we touched upon the most common discussions concerning test automation and sorted out what is good practice and what is not. We also touched upon the history of test-driven development, which has gone through all the phases, from discovery to fundamentalism, and has now arrived at some sort of pragmatism. The next chapter will put testing into the agile context and explore about how it fits into the development process.

8
Testing in an Agile Context

Agile denotes a set of principles supporting methodologies to sustain quality in a software project, even when you have forces pushing the team into taking shortcuts and making sacrifices in order to deliver in a faster and cheaper manner or squeezing in another feature. In the previous chapter, we talked about tools that will help us deliver high-quality products. Now, we will focus on the process that will enable a high-quality project.

Building a bridge or tending to a garden

What is a software project?

It so often happens that building software is compared to construction work. This is a rather strange comparison as construction projects have huge budgets with huge margins for risk. They don't change requirements halfway down the lane. Once the blueprints for a building is complete, there will be no changes during build time, because everything is set in stone.

Errors made in software are also expensive to fix, but instead of having huge margins, software projects are often slimmed down so tightly that there is hardly room for bathroom breaks.

Software projects are nothing at all like construction work. There is this notion that software is more like gardening. The code is the garden that needs to be tended to and grown. If it's not properly taken care of, parts of the garden will fall into decay. This is not really a good observation, as code does not fall into decay if you leave it; it is the rest of the world that changes. The code itself represents the requirements from when it was written, but since then, the business priorities have changed and better languages and tools have emerged.

Software development is more like research and development, where you look at a problem and try to figure out a solution. Seeing it this way, we can derive the following facts:

- What you do not know from the beginning you will learn along the way
- It's not possible to know what is required to solve the problem
- The input requirements for the problem might change along the way

It is hard for businesses to understand this. They don't see the process, the learning, and the research; they see a product that they want and developers as only being there to supply that product. They want to buy the car, but what they're really buying is the process of developing that car. Software development is not a product and it does not have a fixed price.

The broken iron triangle

Businesses would like to know what are getting, for what price, and when they are getting it. This is the most common misconception that ruins quality in all our software projects.

The following diagram is the broken iron triangle:

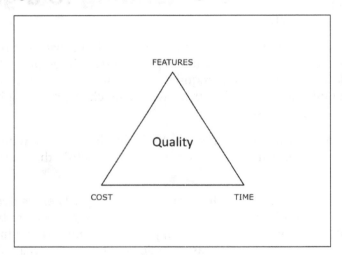

The corners of the triangle represent the three targets you would like to lock down in order to have predictability. However, these are impossible to lock down if you want quality.

Locking down features means deciding on a set of features that should be delivered. This often comes from the client who wants to know what they are getting. The problem, as often shown in agile projects, is that they don't really know what they want before seeing results. Once there is a first demo version of an application, new ideas start popping up and the original scope is not valid anymore.

Locking down cost is done when the client requires a price tag on the system. Trying to estimate the work, a practice that is imprecise, most often requires this. The estimation is turned into a budget, which is then turned into a price tag. You lock down cost at the expense of quality, as no one wants to spend time on a project once the money is gone and with the knowledge that corners will be cut everywhere.

Time represents the deadline and the client asking to have the system ready by a specific date. Once the deadline approaches and the system is not coming along according to plan, it is easy to cut some corners to have it ready in time.

When we talk about fixed price contracts, we always talk about fixed price, fixed deadline, and fixed scope; I want these specific features, for this price, on that date. The only thing you have left to deal with in order to meet these requirements is quality. Cutting on quality will, however, build technical debt, which will cause everything to become slower and more expensive later on.

The proposal Scott Ambler gives us is to lock down two corners of the triangle and keep the third as a variable in order to stay agile.

I was once estimating a development project where the project manager wanted to know how much time it would take in order to provide a client with a budget. The project manager thought my estimates where too high and challenged me on the numbers. I could agree that I wouldn't pay the amount if I were the client, but the estimates where reasonable.

Knowing that this was a fixed price, fixed time, and fixed scope project, I added an extra 20 percent to the total estimate to mitigate the risk of such a project. I told the project manager this and explained why it was needed.

Oh, we usually deduct 20 percent from your estimates in order to sell the proposals to the client. No wonder the projects always go over budget and are never delivered on time.

This book is not about running software projects, but it is about quality, and quality is at the center of these three pillars of software projects. If we don't have a working software development process that will sustain quality in the process, then all other recommendations in this book will be for naught.

Visualizing metrics

The key to software projects is early feedback and creating predictability. This means we can see problems long before they appear and create predictability that will give the team a sustainable pace.

One way of creating predictability is by using the sprint concept from Scrum. Instead of having one long waterfall of specification, implementation, test, and release, you define a three week long time box where you take the highest prioritized features from the backlog and finalize those. This is called a **sprint**, and each sprint is a set of features from the backlog that are most prioritized by the product owner.

The following graph displays a **Sprint burndown chart** from a project I once ran as the Scrum Master:

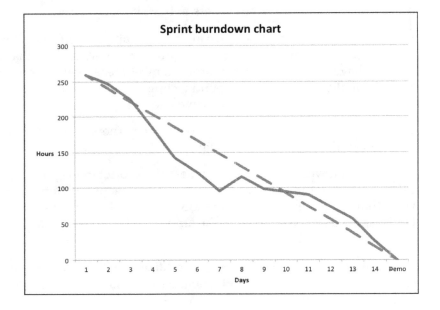

On the Y axis is the amount of work left to do in the sprint, and on the X axis are the number of days until the sprint is finished. On day **7**, there was a sprint refinement meeting where the decision was made to bring in another story from the backlog into the sprint, and that is why hours left in the sprint are increasing.

This chart demonstrates that the sprint is progressing according to plan. It is possible to do the same with the product.

The following graph displays a product burndown chart:

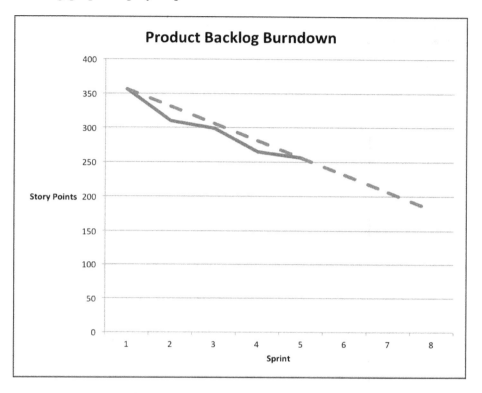

In this chart, the fifth sprint has been committed and it is apparent from the prediction that the whole backlog will not be completed before the eighth sprint. The eighth sprint is the last planned sprint. We have a prediction of how much work can be finished by then. What features might be used is a question of prioritization.

These metrics are important to visualize because they give early feedback on the progress of the project, and make it easier to make decisions that do not reflect poorly on quality.

At the end of the project, when the budget is burned, it is too late to ask the client for more money. At the start of the project, we are still able to revise expectations that all features might not make the decided deadline.

The Kanban board

If you have worked with any kind of agile methodology before, you have likely run across the Kanban board.

The following figure shows a basic example of a Kanban board:

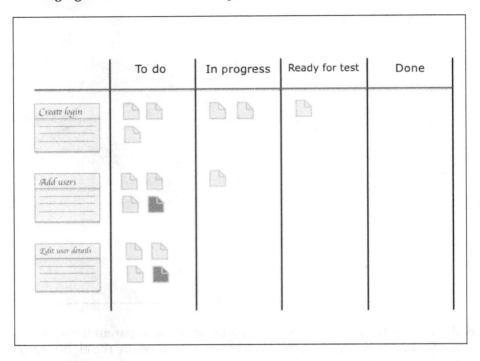

How do we deal with testing and bug reports on the board?

To the left are the user stories that the team has committed to this sprint. The Post-it notes are the user stories broken down into tasks. The columns are the statuses that these tasks are in. When the sprint starts, all the Post-it notes are in the left column, and when the sprint ends, they have all moved to the right.

Testing should be treated just as any other development task, by having a Post-it note for it. When all the other tasks are in the **Ready for test** column, the tester can move his or her task into the **In progress column** and start verification. Any bug found will be added into the **To do** column with a different colored Post-it. It is not necessary to fix all the bugs in order to deliver the sprint, but it is preferable.

When all yellow tasks are in the **Ready for test** column, they can be moved to the **Done column**. The user story is then officially complete. This is very much controlled by the tester.

Predictability

The way to drive software projects within the needle's eye we call the budget is to work out to have as much predictability as possible. Rule out and isolate what is unknown. Divide the project into what's predictable and what's uncertain. Remove unknowns by offering spikes, a time box where you try out new technology, and prestudies outside the project scope.

There are many tools a project manager could use. The following is what we developers can do to create predictability.

Testing

This is how you build a bookcase:

- **Specification**: You start by making a design where you decide how high, wide, and deep the bookcase should be
- **Tests**: You continue by measuring some wood carefully to get the correct length of the parts to be assembled
- **Code**: You hammer it all together, following the design using the carefully assembled parts

Writing a system without specification or tests is like building a bookcase by taking some random parts lying around and hammering them together. It may become something that will hold books, but when the client comes looking, there will be change requests coming. This will continue until the bookcase is good enough to be able to fulfill the original requirements on paper.

The problem here is that you don't know how many iterations it will take to get the feature good enough. The feature will be implemented, tested, bug fixed, tested, and bug fixed again until both developer and tester agree on the result. This is a very unpredictable and expensive way to work.

The following figure shows the workflow of a feature:

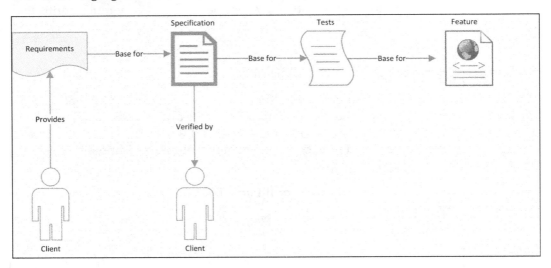

The client, sometimes in conjuncture with the development team, usually creates the requirements. These act as input to the specification that is created by the team and verified by the client. The specifications act as inputs to the tests. When all the tests are green, the feature is completely implemented.

This is then done for each and every feature on the backlog, as long as the software project is active. It is this practice that creates a sustainable pace and predictability.

It is never a good idea to try creating the full specification of a system before the software project is started. This neglects the fact that software development is a learning process and that the specifications will change once development has started.

What it means to be done

What is very important for predictability in a software project is knowing when a feature is done. This can be harder than it seems. Before starting a project, the team should make a definition of what it means to be done with a feature:

- The feature should be function-tested
- The feature should have automated tests
- The feature should be reviewed
- The feature should be documented

Before a feature can be moved to the **Done** column on the Kanban board, all these definitions of **Done** should be fulfilled. Even if the definition is clear, it is easy to skip these definitions when a project is getting stressed. This is the same as rounding corners on quality and building technical debt.

In order to make sure the definition of **Done** is not taken lightly, it is important to add it as tasks to each story of the sprint. It becomes much harder to cheat the definition of **Done** when developers have to confirm it is done by moving the task on the Kanban board.

Mitigating risks

Predictability means we know what is going on. We take what we have and create a plan. We measure and visualize in order to get constant feedback for our process. The way to assess the greatest risks to our projects lies in knowing:

- What we know
- What we know that we don't know
- What we don't know that we don't know

We call them **known knowns**, **known unknowns**, and **unknown unknowns**.

What we know is what we use when estimating a project, creating a project plan, and building a backlog. This is what we make our assumptions on and what we present to the client. It is everything else that is our dark mass in the project universe.

Known unknowns

The known unknowns are what we use to manage risk within our project. In our estimates, we add a little time because we have a known unknown. We add a few days to the delivery date because of the uncertainties.

An example of known unknowns is integration with a third part, which we never have done before. It could be a framework or language that the developers have no previous experience of, or a dependency to a design bureau. Ultimately, it could be anything we know beforehand that might cause us a delay.

How to deal with known unknowns is often quite straightforward. We can provide more time in the schedule for hard integration. We could have the developers make a spike on that new framework in order to learn, or send them on a course to learn the new language. We could provide the design bureau one set of deadlines and use more generous deadlines toward the client.

The known unknowns represent risk we can mitigate and expenses that go beyond what a project would normally cost if there where no known unknowns.

Unknown unknowns

The unknown unknowns are things we couldn't anticipate in the software project. The framework the application is developed with won't work on the production environment. Far into the project, legalities will restrict you from using a core component because it is open source under a license you can't support. When drafting out specifications, you will find that two major requirements are contradicting one another.

The only way to mitigate the unknown unknowns is to leave room in the project for unforeseeable things. We don't know beforehand how much space is needed, as we don't know that we don't know. We just have to come up with an index that is decent enough to continue the project, even if the unknown happens.

An unknown factor might change the rules of the project completely, and one should not be afraid to cancel a project if it's not viable to carry it out. It's better to lose the initial investment than carry on creating something that will be obsolete before hitting the market. You will always leave a project with experiences and knowledge that you didn't have before.

Automation

Continuous integration is the practice of having a build server running a series of operations on the code as soon as it is committed to the source code repository.

The tasks most often performed in the build server are:

- Compiling the code looking for lexical errors
- Executing any automated tests (unit tests, integration tests)
- Running static code analysis on the code
- Running linting tools to verify code style

The point of this is to verify that the committed code is acceptable to the quality standards initially set up by the project.

This following figure shows the workflow of continuous integration:

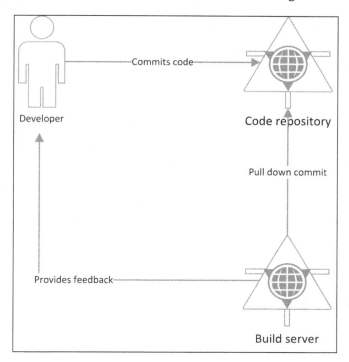

The reason for this practice is that integrating your code with other developers is hurtful, and a way to mitigate that pain is to do it more often. In the same spirit, a practice called continuous deployment has emerged, mitigating the pain of deploying code to production.

The following workflow shows how continuous integration hooks into continuous deployment:

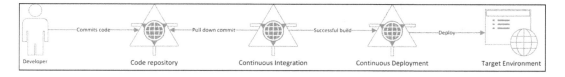

The point here is when the code has been tested, it is verified to be deployable by continuous integration; that process carries over to continuous deployment, which makes sure code is delivered to target environments.

The point of both continuous integration and continuous deployment is to get instant feedback on submitted work and create a predictable working environment where the path from code to live feature is shorter and easier traveled.

When the CI/CD workflow is failing by a test not turning green, it should be the team's top priority to get it back to green. This will otherwise disturb the whole operation and if that process is allowed to stay red for a longer time, chances are that when it's truly needed, it is not possible to get it back to green.

With these conclusions, we must try to create predictability in our software projects, and one way to do so is to work with test automation, a clear definition of done, automating code integration and deployment, and also understanding what we know, what we don't know, and dealing with what we don't know that we don't know.

Testing in agile

When testing in agile development, it can be hard to know where in the process testing fits in. This differs depending on what kind of testing it is.

The following figure illustrates testing that has commenced in an agile process:

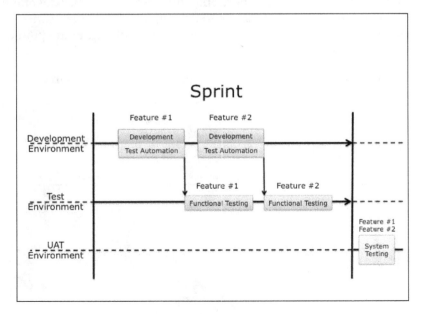

There is testing that should be confined in the sprint and then testing that will happen after the sprint.

When the developer is working on a feature, he or she will also develop the automatic tests for that feature, making sure he or she has the feature covered with tests. This will make the job of the tester easier, as this individual can focus on investigating the feature and not so much on checking the requirements. It will also reduce the number of turnarounds between development and functional testing. The feature gets function-tested during the sprint. There are important aspects to this:

- Functional testing should have its own stable test environment
- All deployments to test the environment have a discrete version such as 1.1.1234
- The tester controls when deployment to test the environment is done
- The last feature in the sprint must not be finished too late to allow room for functional testing

When it is time for demo, the code of the sprint is deployed to a demo environment where it can be reviewed by the business. This is also where any kind of system testing is applied, such as load testing, stress testing, security testing, and so on.

The following figure shows what happens when a bug is found by functional testing:

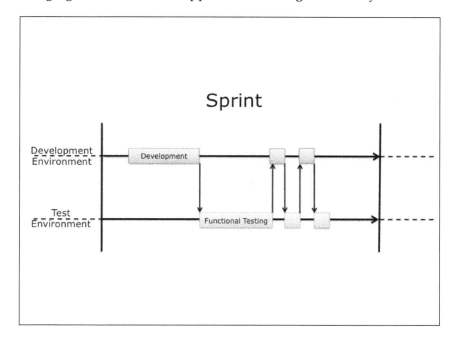

The problems here are obvious. The bug reports that come back from functional testing disrupt the feature development. There is overhead in the back and forth between development and testing, which makes the process of fixing bugs costly and tiresome. As the client that suggested we do it right the first time, this is exactly what should be sought to achieve with test automation, as fixing bugs from functional testing is too costly.

In sprint planning, you very seldom make room in the sprint for bug fixing the features. It will be handled by any remaining space in the sprint after all the features are done. Bugs not fixed in the sprint can be planned to be fixed in the next sprint. That is why you often deliver a sprint with known issues.

It is important that bugs are not fixed at the end of the sprint, but everly divided on the sprint. The key is to provide the tester with work to do by following these steps:

1. Fix planned bugs from the previous sprint at the start of the sprint, to have the tester verify the fixes.
2. Pick up reported bugs between features. When one feature is done, before starting work on the next, check if there are any open bugs to fix.
3. Bugs fixed late in the sprint will most likely be added as planned bugs to the next sprint.

Summary

In order to begin performing quality practices such as testing in a software project, the software project must first enable those practices by being in good health. You need an agile project that embraces change instead of preventing it. You need a product owner that understands that requirements changes, and management that sees that a plan is not equal to the reality. The team members of the project must understand the value of predictability and the value of doing quality work like test automation.

In this chapter, we've discussed what a developer must know about software projects in order to perform test automation. In the next chapter, we'll talk about test smells, or anti-patterns as they're also called (which are the most common ones), and how we are going to avoid them.

9
Test Smells

A code smell is a symptom in the code that possibly indicates a deeper problem. It's where we look and think that there must be a better way of doing this. Tests also smell but they smell when they are run. There are different kinds of test smells and I will use the following method on these smells:

- What is it?
- How did it come to be?
- What to do about it?

After reading this chapter, you will be able to identify test smells at an early stage and fight them in order to keep a good and healthy test suite.

Tests that break upon refactoring

One very common test smell when dealing with unit tests is that your tests break when you refactor, even though the functionality stays the same. These kinds of tests are called **brittle** tests.

There are two kinds of breaks:

- Your test suite doesn't compile after refactoring
- Your test suite still compiles, but no longer turns green

Tests would stop compiling if you change the external API the test is relying on. If that is part of your refactoring, then the compilation error is okay and expected. If you're changing the internal implementation of your functionality, then the test should not be affected and still compile.

A test that fails to compile after refactoring could be a sign of testing in a too granular level and testing implementation details instead of testing the function as a whole.

If your test suite still compiles after refactoring but your test fails, you have the same root problem. You're testing on a too granular abstraction level. This is a common case when using mocking that knows too much about how parts of the system interact with other parts. When that implementation detail changes, the test will break, even though the functionality stays the same.

This is also the reason why many unit test advocates also preach to us to stay away from mocks, as they have us testing things that are too close to implementation-level details.

This kind of problem usually comes from writing the test last, after the implementation, as it is then much easier to write tests that cover the code that was written than writing tests that cover the feature that was developed.

As a developer, you can use several tools in order to avoid this test smell:

- Do TDD and write tests first
- Write your tests as user stories
- Don't use mocking frameworks

Lastly, don't use coverage tools that will make you look at a percentage of the covered number, instead of the testing problem in front of you.

Tests that break occasionally

One of the most common test smells are tests that break from time to time. Sometimes you have a test that breaks once and then never again. Other tests will always fail the first time and then succeed when they're rerun. It often happens that you write a test that will work perfectly now but fail sometime in the future.

When it comes to unit testing, this kind of test smell is quite rare. Since your unit tests should operate on memory only, there are few things that would make the test fail occasionally. One thing would be threading. A race condition is always the kind of test that would break when the CPU cycles don't perform in the expected order. This could cause the test to fail even though it is a unit test.

It is much more common that integration tests have occasional hiccups. There could be a dip in the network during database transaction, or the hard drive that you're writing logs to is full. These are things that we have a hard time to protect ourselves from, as it is not the responsibility of the test to check for these things.

Tests that will always fail the first time and succeed in the second are caused because of bad timing. One common example of this would be tests timing out because the application pool is still restarting after a successful deploy.

Another mistake is to disregard caching, where a test would fail at the first try but succeed in the second because the second time the cache has been filled with everything that was needed for the test to succeed.

In the same manner, a large test suite might create a state that will help other tests to pass or fail. Running a test individually is not the same as running it as part of a test suite, as it is very seldom for each test run to clear all states and run with a clean state. There will always be a state that can make your tests pass or fail.

The danger of this test smell is that we stop trusting the test suite when it fails for no apparent reason. If the test suite is always red, then we will not go to it for a status check whether the system is healthy or not. Then, the test suite stops delivering its promised value.

The following actions can be taken to avoid this test smell:

- Avoid testing threaded code. Test the individual parts in a single threaded state.
- Try isolating the test as best you can by clearing all the states from previous tests.
- Make sure that SUT is prepared when you run your test suite. If you have been deploying code to an **Internet Information Services (IIS)** website just before, make sure you warm it up.

If a test is failing often because the circumstances around the test causes it to fail, then it would be a better idea to remove that test than letting it devalue your whole test suite.

Your test suite should always be green, with only passing tests. If there is one test that is misbehaving and occasionally turning red, it is better to delete that test. A test suite must be trusted by the developers, and it can't be trusted if it often turns red.

Tests that never break

Another common smell is tests that never break, no matter how much you break the feature. This is quite common to see in unit tests where tests are written after the system under test. The test itself is there to cover some part of the code to bring the coverage up, but it is disconnected from the feature that it is actually covering.

What is common for all these tests is that there is a bug in the test that makes it pass even when the result is wrong. Writing bugs in tests is quite common and should never be underestimated. Another common reason is that the test has been badly named and is not actually asserting the thing it is named after. This will result in green, passing tests when the thing the test was supposed to verify is actually failing.

This is the test that you will find when looking for a bug. The test will claim to cover for the bug you've found, but the test will pass, even though the problem obviously is there. In the end, you will find that the test itself has a bug, and in order to expose it, you must first fix the bug in the test.

The problem with these tests is that they bring no value, as they do not verify that the feature is working. In contrary, the test is dangerous, as it provides a false sense of security that 100 percent coverage would mean the features are 100 percent bug-free.

This is how you can avoid this smell:

- Make sure your test is always red before it's green
- Don't write tests in order to bring up code coverage
- Ensure that you're asserting exactly what you've named the test after

If you find a test that will not fail, you should fix the test so it starts providing value, or you should remove it from the test suite. Otherwise, it is just there for you to brag about how many tests or the amount of code coverage you have. This is just a waste and doesn't bring any value.

Tests that are too complex

If you cannot see what the test is about at a glance, then it is too complex. The first thing you look at is the name of the test, which should tell you what the test is asserting, and the second is the implementation of the test, which should be a few lines of straightforward code.

The signs of a too complex test are as follows:

- Large amount of setup code needed
- Conditional logic, such as `if`, `switch`, or null-coalescing operators are used
- Looping constructs, such as `while`, `for`, or `foreach` are used
- The test needs helper functions or types to operate
- It has more than one mock or stub
- It requires mocking and stubbing more than one method or property
- The test doesn't fit the screen without scrolling

When the test fails, the developer looking at the test might not be the same that wrote it from the start. This makes it imperative that the test itself is as straightforward as possible. Even more plausible, the developer looking at the test is not even very familiar with the system, and looking at the tests should help that developer to understand the system under test and not make it more complicated.

The most common reason for ending up with complex tests is that you have a system that is hard to test. If you have the sole responsibility for such systems, then you can only blame yourself for not designing code with testability.

Sometimes it is hard to control if you depend on a framework that in itself is difficult to test. The most common example would be ASP.NET, which has become better with the latest versions but still poses a challenge while dealing with states such as cookies, sessions, and redirects.

There are things we can do in order to produce simpler tests, as follows:

- Use TDD test first. This will let you design for testability by writing the test first.
- Stay away from frameworks that make testing harder.
- SOLID principles will bring you far, but composition over inheritance is crucial to reduce coupling.
- Stop writing the test when it starts to smell and start refactoring the SUT instead.

A test that breaks and is too complex for the developer to fix should be deleted. This means that complex tests devalue your test suite and should be avoided. Once we get practice in testing, writing simple tests will come more naturally to us, and it will become easier to produce good and fresh test suites.

Tests that require excessive setup

A slight indication that your system under test is too complex is that the test setup becomes excessive. The easiest way to identify this is when you have 20 lines of setup code in order to run one line of test code. Some of it you might also need to tear down after the test is complete.

The test itself doesn't have to be very complex, but the complexity of the system under test forces the excessive setup on the test. What often happens is that this setup is duplicated from test to tests, causing a lot of duplicated code. The most commonly seen solution is then to extract the method once the test is set up, but this is really bad. Instead, the problem should be addressed in the system under test.

The excessive setup code is usually as follows:

* Setup of dependencies necessary to execute the test
* Setup of states necessary to execute the test

In most modern systems, there is a dependency injection framework in the middle that handles dependencies through the system. This is because object orientation is flawed in a way that requires the developer to create large object graphs in order to perform a simple thing. These object graphs are created and managed by the dependency injection framework so the developer can request an instance of a specific type in the system and have the framework worry about the dependencies.

When writing unit tests, you often want to exchange the dependencies for your own stubs. Commonly, you want to exchange dependencies that are indirect and a few levels down the sub tree, and not only the direct dependencies you input when creating the class manually.

This leads us to the major parts of the test setup: managing the dependency injection framework to exchange the dependencies that you need and then resetting the **Dependency Injection (DI)** framework in the tear down, because the DI framework is often a singleton in the system and shared throughout the test suite's execution.

So, what can we do about excessive test setup? We can do the following:

* Reduce the dependency graph in the system under test
* Avoid relying on global states such as singletons or thread states such as session data
* Design your APIs to be easy to set up, and use conventions where all options are not mandatory
* When writing a test that requires excessive setup, stop and refactor SUT

The danger with having tests with lots of setup code is that the tests then become hard to read and there is an extract method on the setup code instead of a method that would help us deal with the problem in the system under test. There is also a potential waste: making a change to the dependencies of the SUT will cause a lot of maintenance in the test suite, as all the test setups would then need to be revised to have the test suite compile again. This will become a large time sink in the project and a major waste.

Developers not writing tests

The largest problem your test suite will have is developers that won't write tests. If there is a test suite and the test is run upon committing new code, then the tests will run when these developers commit code to the repository. However, the new code will not be covered by tests and there is uncertainty as to what will happen if the commit breaks the existing tests. Will the developer fix these tests or leave the test suite red?

The impact of not writing tests will start to devalue the whole test suite as the coverage goes down. If some developers stop updating the test suites, then others will follow, and soon you will have a test suite without any active development. Then, the team will not get full benefits, such as enabling refactoring or feeling safe about new features.

I have experienced development teams disabling a whole test suite because a test was failing. They claimed it was because they needed a green build in order to deploy to production. The reason they were talking to me was that the deploy they did had critical errors in it they didn't know how to fix. My first suggestion to them was to re-enable the test suite and make the tests pass.

The question it boils down to is why aren't these developers writing tests? I did some asking around and boiled it down to these answers:

- Testing is a waste
- Management won't let us
- We don't know where to start
- Our code is too hard to test
- It's a thing about culture

All of these issues come from developers that haven't practiced testing in their day-to-day work. They may have learned about it and know that it is a better way doing software development, but they don't have the extra motivation to start writing tests.

Testing is a waste

There is a certain type of programmer that is reluctant to change, and every proposal of different work methods will result in fierce resistance. The uninformed developer will claim that all time not spent on writing features is a waste. The informed developer will know that spending time on test will cause us to spend even less time on building features, and we will gain from it in the long run by delivering higher quality code that is less buggy.

The only way of getting around this mentality is to pair up and show how easy it is to start writing tests. Once you have some green tests to feel good about, the resistance will eventually die down.

Management won't let us

Project managers have one foot standing in the client's ballpark and the other in development. They need to engage the clients and make promises that they know are not possible and that they will have a hard time keeping them. As project managers are often placed above the team in the hierarchy, the manager will force the team to deliver on their promises. This is one of the most common reasons that managers don't let a team engage in quality measures, as they will always hunt for the next promised deadline.

It's like building a card castle that will eventually fall apart, and this is why we prefer working in agile cross-functional teams.

If you can't fire management for not letting you do your job, then it is time to look for a new one. There are enough good jobs around that it's a shame to stay with a bad one.

We don't know where to start

I've been doing lots of tutoring on test-driven development, and even when coming out from a 2-hour long seminar on TDD, developers will open up a code editor and just stare blankly at the screen for minutes because they can't come up with a good name for their first test. This happens to everyone, and is part of the learning curve in order to become a testing developer.

A good solution I've found is to pair up with developers that are new to testing and help them out with some backseat driving. Just helping them to reason out what is considered a good test name will take them a good way down the path to test automation.

Our code is hard to test

Most systems aren't that resilient to test automation. In almost all situations, you will be able to isolate parts of the system that are hard to test and focus testing on the core functionality, where the impact is the most valuable. If you are new and insecure about testing, then denial is a natural reaction.

The easiest way to get around this is to have the junior testing developer pair up with a senior and sort out the problems by testing a particular system. Most of the time, there will be an easy way to get around the most common obstacles.

It's a thing about culture

What you need is a testing culture, where it is natural for all the developers in the team to engage in testing activities. By having a strong testing culture, there will never be a doubt about what to test.

You can build a testing culture by convincing your team that everything should be tested. Build up the confidence in the team around testing, and then it will start to spread around the company. Other teams will envy your successes and start adopting your methods and processes, and soon you will grow your very own testing culture.

Summary

We have been looking at different test smells that indicate that there is something wrong with your test suite, with your test process, or with the competence or motivation of your testing developers.

The important factor when doing test automation is to never forget what you're doing and why you are doing it. While writing the test number 2,501 in the suite, it can be difficult to remember that the test helps you design your system. It will provide regression so you avoid fixing problems that you've already fixed. Lastly, it will help you gain quality in your application, which reduces the total number of bugs to fix in the first place.

In the next chapter, I will close this book with some thoughts on dos and don'ts when it comes to test automation. This will help you succeed in scaling large test suites.

10

The Ten Commandments of Test Automation

In this last chapter, we're going to look at some of the learning we have found along the way, condensed in a format of Ten Commandments. As it is easier to learn high-quality coding looking at anti-patterns on what you should not do, in the same way it is easier to start writing good tests by telling what you shouldn't do. By adding restrictions on testing, you'll find your tests becoming purer and you will start writing test suites that are easier to maintain and provide more value.

Testing behavior, not implementation

```
// don't
[<Test>]
let ``should hash user password with SHA1`` () =
    () // test body

// do
[<Test>]
let ``should hash user password to make it unreadable`` () =
    ()
```

Unless **hash algorithm** is an explicit requirement, it should be considered an implementation detail.

You should never go down to a level of abstraction where your test expresses what the system should do. Instead, you should always test on what the feature expects of the system. The difference is that a test focusing on implementation will break on refactoring, whereas a test that focuses on behavior will not. Safe refactoring is one major part to why we're writing tests in the first place; so, we should really try to support this as much as we can.

This means that we don't explicitly test private methods, constructors, initializers, or patterns, unless they are backed up by a user story.

Using ubiquitous language in your test name

Let us take a look at the following code:

```
// don't
[<Test>]
let ``store transaction to database`` () =
    ()

// do
[<Test>]
let ``when customer checkout the cart, the order is persisted`` () =
    ()
```

Use words and expressions from the domain when expressing test names.

Getting the naming right is one of the hardest parts for the new tester. Before you know how to name your test, you need to know what to test, and before you know what to test you need to know what the feature is all about.

A good test name should state something about the feature, so obvious that a business analyst would agree with it. The test name should also reflect on what we're asserting.

In order to achieve this, I usually start my test names with the should word, and let the fixture hold the name of the feature as follows:

- when submitting the form.should warn about invalid e-mail address
- when submitting the form.should store the user profile to database

The first part is the name of the feature we're testing and the last part is the name of the test. When it comes to testing for exceptions I usually exchange the `should` word for `cannot` but keep the format.

Asserting only one thing in your test

Let us take a look at the following code:

```
// don't
[<Test>]
let ``username and password cannot be empty string`` () =
    // arrange
    let credentials = Credentials(System.String.Empty, System.String.
Empty)

    // act
    let result = validate(credentials)

    // assert
    result |> should contain UserNameEmpty
    result |> should contain PasswordEmpty

// do
[<Test>]
let ``username cannot be empty string`` () =
    // arrange
    let credentials = Credentials(System.String.Empty, "secret")

    // act
    let result = validate(credentials)

    // assert
    result |> should contain UserNameEmpty

// do
[<Test>]
let ``password cannot be empty string`` () =
    // arrange
    let credentials = Credentials("user", System.String.Empty)

    // act
    let result = validate(credentials)

    // assert
    result |> should contain PasswordEmpty
```

Cohesion in your code means that the function will do one and only one thing. This is easier when it comes to functional programming languages as you have the whole pure functional pattern and one function should always yield the same result for the same input.

When it comes to tests, cohesion also applies. One test should only test one thing. The cases where this rule is broken are where you have several asserts in the end. The use of asserting more than one thing is often a case of bad cohesion.

It is very important to have high cohesion in your test so that you know why the test failed. When you have several asserts in the same test and the test fails, you don't know from a glance what assert made the test break. Instead, you're looking at the name of the test to determine what functionality broke.

This comes down to good naming and good scoping of your tests. A more generic name of your test will invite several asserts to verify that the test passes. A more specific naming convention will only require one assert to verify the test outcome. With this, we should have narrow test targets with good naming conventions that will produce only one assert at the end of the test.

At times, there are situations where you need several asserts in the same test, even though you've scoped the test well and named it from an explicit requirement. This is when you're breaking the rule, and you know that you're breaking the rule.

Don't mock the Mockingbird

Let us take a look at the following code:

```
// don't
[<Test>]
let ``should first get customers from customer service and then store
them to hard drive`` () =
    // arrange
    let customerService = MockRepository.GenerateMock<ICustomerServi
ce>()
    let fileSystem = MockRepository.GenerateMock<IFileSystem>()
    let cacheJob = CacheJob(customerService, fileSystem)

    // setup mocks
    customerService.Expect(fun service -> service.GetCustomers()).
Return([(1, "Mikael Lundin")]) |> ignore
    fileSystem.Expect(fun fs -> fs.AppendLineToFile("customer.txt",
"1,Mikael Lundin")) |> ignore

    // act
```

```
cacheJob.Execute() |> ignore

// assert
customerService.VerifyAllExpectations()
fileSystem.VerifyAllExpectations()

// do
// simplify the SUT or implement a vertical slice
```

What if we change the storage from filesystem to database? Should the test fail when implementation changes?

Mocks aren't evil, but they are very often the root source for brittle tests. Mocking in the sense of recording what will happen on the unit's dependencies and return fake results means that your test knows what dependencies the unit is having and in what sense it interacts with these. The test knows too much about the implementation of the system.

Fake dependencies are okay, in the sense that we can send in a fake object to the unit that we're testing, in order to fake a state on the program and this way test the expected results. Stubs are such that we fill a fake object with data and let the unit under test operate on this stub. The problem with mocks is that we put expectations on interactions between part of the system and this breaks when we're refactoring the code.

In the end, this is as bad as testing private functions, as they are both internal workings of the system's implementation.

The exception to this rule is when you want to test the interaction with an external system without making it an integration test. If you're implementing an **Object Relational Mapper (ORM)** and want to test what kind of SQL is generated for the database, a mock could be in place unless you can get that SQL in any other way.

Always refactor your SUT

In the testing pattern red, green, refactor the last part is often forgotten. Once the test goes green, it is easy for the developer to forget about the refactoring part, or just move on because of a pressing deadline.

The refactoring part is the most important part of testing as this is what makes our code high-quality. Some of our system code is very hard to test and will not be enabled for test automation until we have refactored it. It is therefore crucial to refactor after each test so that we don't build technical debt.

One of the greater points of unit testing is to enable refactoring. By having coverage over your features, you will ensure that nothing gets broken after the refactoring is complete. Refactoring is the art of changing the dinner table cloth with all the plates still standing on the table, and to enable that you need to have a test suite to keep you covered.

Writing tests is a way of designing your code, and this is why testing and refactoring go hand in hand. You should let your tests put requirements on the design of your code, and drive this design. It might be possible to retrofit tests on an existing design without changing anything, but then you're missing out on one of the true benefits of test-driven development.

Your test should never be more than 10 lines of code

Here is one controversial commandment that always takes my students aback when I'm teaching them test-driven development. In F#, this is not a hard requirement and in C# it only brings a healthy restriction on the length of a test.

Because the length of a test is directly proportional with how readable this test is. A longer test will be less readable, and the longer it is the harder it will be to maintain. Instead, I propose that we should have as short tests as possible. The optimal length of a test would be three lines of code. We have the triple A syntax pattern as follows:

- Arrange
- Act
- Assert

Sometimes, you need a few more lines of arrange, in order to set up the prerequisites for the test to run. Assert might need an extra line to help extract the result we got from running the test.

The act section of the test should always be only one line of code. This is important to keep the test cohesive. If the act only consists of one line of code, then we know that we're only testing one thing.

If the test as a whole is more than 10 lines of code, then our SUT is too complex and we should refactor it in order to bring complexity down. Long tests are a great test smell indicating that there is an underlying problem.

Not only leading to tests that are hard to maintain, but also having long tests will give the developer an urge to dry it up, by extracting method on the arrange part and having all the tests calling a setup method. This is a really bad idea as it breaks the test apart and makes it even harder to maintain. This refactoring of the test may, however, be closer at hand than doing a major refactoring of the SUT.

Always test in isolation

A good test is one that is completely confined within the function where it is defined. The state of the test suite and the state of the system are the same after the test has run, as it was before.

When tests are not isolated, you start to get maintenance and reliability problems. The most common refactoring that developers do on their test suite is to share setup between tests. It is common that tests share much of the setup code, but instead it should be considered a waste. Instead, we need to investigate how we can refactor the SUT in order to avoid excessive and repeatable tests setup. Once we've done this, we will end up with better tests and better-designed SUT.

Tests need not only to be isolated from each other by code, but also by state. One of the largest problems in test suites is that one test sets a particular state in the target system and this affects the results of subsequent tests. These bugs are hard to track down because the error is not in the test that is failing. Even worse, these bugs are seldom due to a fault in the actual system but only in the test suite, which makes every minute chasing these bugs a waste, unless you will end up reducing the need for state in the SUT.

It is quite common to set up a common state for several tests, and then tear it down when the test fixture is done. This is often done because the setup is a slow process that requires a lot of time. If it is done only once instead of 50 times, you can speed up the test suite substantially. The problem is that these tests will operate on the common state, and may inflict the appearances of a bug, where it was just due to tests changing a state that is not even possible in the system under testing.

In every situation, we should strive for isolating each test so that they don't touch upon other tests or their test runs. This is a Utopian idea and not always appropriate. We need to weigh our options to have a potentially brittle test suite that breaks when you remove a test, because the subsequent tests were depending on its state or having a test suite that takes hours to execute because each test needs to reset the whole application domain before performing one assertion.

We need to be pragmatic, and we need to know what is wrong and why we choose to do it anyway.

Controlling your dependencies

Control your dependencies before they take control of you. If you have a unit test where you need to stub out three dependencies, then you're spending more time dealing with the coupling of the SUT than actually testing that it's doing in the right thing. Dependencies are a huge problem in programming and something that needs to be dealt with very carefully.

When you're using a dependency injection framework, you're making life easy for yourself by letting the framework create your object and all its dependencies. This means that there is no problem for you to add more and more dependencies to the class under test, because there is no punishment for doing so. Not until you start writing tests.

When you're writing tests, you can tolerate one dependency of your unit, but not more than this. This is why your SUT needs to be abstracted so that one unit never has more than one dependency. This will make your code easier to read and follow. The downside is that the dependency graph will become deeper and it might get harder to understand the big picture of your system if you're not managing this dependency graph appropriately.

One way of dealing with the dependency graph is vertical slice testing where you exchange only the most outbound layers of your application with fake. The filesystem is a fake filesystem, the web service is a fake web service, and the database is a fake database. This way, there will be no need to deal with dependencies in your tests, as all functionalities will only be called in memory anyway.

Your test is a ninja

The reason that your test fails should be exact because it doesn't fulfill the promise of how the test is named. There should be no other reason for the test to fail, and it should be given no chance of failing because of anything else.

In many cases, we need to run a lot of code in order to get to the state that we want to test. This is a potential problem, because the code that we're passing through might fail and give us a failing test, but for a completely other reason than why the test was written. This is bad, because it makes the test suite hard to understand and hard to bug trace.

The only way to get around this problem is to limit the amount of code needed in order to run our tests, and that we can only do by refactoring the SUT. Bring in a state record that can be sent into the routine that we want to test and fake. This is one way to shorten the path to our unit. Another way is to reduce dependencies and reduce the size of the function. Often, we have to deal with this issue because the SUT has low cohesion, meaning that the function that we want to test provides more than one service.

A good rule when writing unit tests is to be in and out as quickly as possible, making a small imprint as possible. In order to enable this, we will often have to refactor the SUT.

The test is not complex

You should avoid complexity in your test at all costs. A few lines of straightforward workflow should be enough for arrange, act, and assert.

This means that we disallow the following in our tests:

- Conditional statements such as `if`, `match`, and `function`
- Looping constructs such as `while`, `for`
- Additional types, interfaces, discriminated unions, or classes apart from the SUT
- Threads
- Exception handling, except asserting for thrown exceptions
- Manipulation of lists, sequences, maps, or tuples

In short, your test should be as simple as the following steps:

1. Set up the prerequisites to run the test.
2. Run the test.
3. Assert the result.

If anything else is needed, you probably have a too complex system that needs refactoring in order to bring down the complexity of your tests. Complexity in your tests will hurt you in several different ways. The most common is that your test will fail even before touching the SUT because the initialization logic assumes conditions of the SUT that might change during refactoring.

Fixing a complex test takes time, because it takes time to understand the test. Most often, it is better to delete a failing complex test than trying to fix it. Even if its fixed, there is a high probability that it will fail soon again.

This leads us to the complexity of the test making it cost more than you actually gain in value. This means that we shouldn't write tests that are complex. Instead, we should stop in our tracks and ask ourselves how we can refactor the SUT in order to avoid the complexity.

Summary

In this chapter, we have been looking at the Ten Commandments for writing good test suites. Following these Ten Commandments is hard. It is a struggle to work with the limitations in order to produce even better test suites that provide more value than they cost. But if you follow these commandments, you will be falling into the pit of success, making it a struggle to fail.

This concludes the end of this book. We have been looking into how you can benefit from F# when writing high-quality code that is covered by tests. I have been showing how functional programming plays into the unit testing role and how we can benefit from the paradigm in order to make our test suites stronger and more robust.

I hope that you have enjoyed reading this book as much as I have enjoyed writing it, and I hope that you found it valuable in your path to great test suites and bug-free applications.

Index

G

GetUsers() method 127
Gherkin 22, 180
Git 84
Git Hooks 84
Global Assembly Cache (GAC) 153

H

hash algorithm 253
helper functions 116
higher order functions 40, 126

I

IDisposable 10
ilspy 51
immutability
  about 29
  benefits 29
immutable data structures 31
immutable type
  creating 37, 38
imperative programming 46
inline tests
  versus separate project 95-97
integration testing
  in parallel 159-162
  speeding up 159
integration tests
  about 11, 141, 142
  external interface testing 145
  layer-for-layer testing 143
  limitations 142
  top down testing 144
  writing 145-148
intent
  testing with 16
Intermediate Language (IL) 51
Internet Information Services (IIS) 245

J

JetBrains 85

K

Kanban board
  example 234

L

lambdas 125
large databases
  setting up 155-158
layer-for-layer testing 143
layer-for-layer tests
  writing 143
let keyword 29
Lines of Code (LOC) 30
Lisp 33
list type
  about 33
  advantages 34
  properties 34
Luhn 35

M

manual testing 8, 9
MatchConstraint() function 102
Matches() method 102
method injection 123
metrics
  visualizing 232, 233
mocking 132-136
Model View Controller (MVC) 107
MSTest 69
MSTest tests
  running, outside Visual Studio 75, 76
mutable state
  used, for implementing String.Join
    function 29, 30

N

NCover 217
NCrunch 142
NuGet package manager 10
NUnit 64, 69, 71
NUnit tests
  running, outside Visual Studio 76-78
  running, within Visual Studio 64-66

X

Thank you for buying
Testing with F#

About Packt Publishing

Packt, pronounced 'packed', published its first book, *Mastering phpMyAdmin for Effective MySQL Management*, in April 2004, and subsequently continued to specialize in publishing highly focused books on specific technologies and solutions.

Our books and publications share the experiences of your fellow IT professionals in adapting and customizing today's systems, applications, and frameworks. Our solution-based books give you the knowledge and power to customize the software and technologies you're using to get the job done. Packt books are more specific and less general than the IT books you have seen in the past. Our unique business model allows us to bring you more focused information, giving you more of what you need to know, and less of what you don't.

Packt is a modern yet unique publishing company that focuses on producing quality, cutting-edge books for communities of developers, administrators, and newbies alike. For more information, please visit our website at www.packtpub.com.

About Packt Open Source

In 2010, Packt launched two new brands, Packt Open Source and Packt Enterprise, in order to continue its focus on specialization. This book is part of the Packt Open Source brand, home to books published on software built around open source licenses, and offering information to anybody from advanced developers to budding web designers. The Open Source brand also runs Packt's Open Source Royalty Scheme, by which Packt gives a royalty to each open source project about whose software a book is sold.

Writing for Packt

We welcome all inquiries from people who are interested in authoring. Book proposals should be sent to author@packtpub.com. If your book idea is still at an early stage and you would like to discuss it first before writing a formal book proposal, then please contact us; one of our commissioning editors will get in touch with you.

We're not just looking for published authors; if you have strong technical skills but no writing experience, our experienced editors can help you develop a writing career, or simply get some additional reward for your expertise.

F# for Quantitative Finance

ISBN: 978-1-78216-462-3   Paperback: 286 pages

An introductory guide to utilizing F# for quantitative finance leveraging the .NET platform

1. Learn functional programming with an easy-to-follow combination of theory and tutorials.

2. Build a complete automated trading system with the help of code snippets.

3. Use F# Interactive to perform exploratory development.

4. Leverage the .NET platform and other existing tools from Microsoft using F#.

Windows Phone 7.5 Application Development with F#

ISBN: 978-1-84968-784-3   Paperback: 138 pages

Develop amazing applications for Windows Phone using F#

1. Understand the Windows Phone application development environment and F# as a language.

2. Discover how to work with Windows Phone controls using F#.

3. Learn how to work with gestures, navigation, and data access.

Please check **www.PacktPub.com** for information on our titles

Learning Software Testing with Test Studio

ISBN: 978-1-84968-890-1   Paperback: 376 pages

Embark on the exciting journey of test automation, execution, and reporting in Test Studio with this practical tutorial

1. Learn to use Test Studio to design and automate tests valued with their functionality and maintainability.

2. Run manual and automated test suites and view reports on them.

3. Filled with practical examples, snapshots and Test Studio hints to automate and substitute throwaway tests with long term frameworks.

Advanced Penetration Testing for Highly-Secured Environments: The Ultimate Security Guide

ISBN: 978-1-84951-774-4   Paperback: 414 pages

Learn to perform professional penetration testing for highly-secured environments with this intensive hands-on guide

1. Learn how to perform an efficient, organized, and effective penetration test from start to finish.

2. Gain hands-on penetration testing experience by building and testing a virtual lab environment that includes commonly found security measures such as IDS and firewalls.

Please check **www.PacktPub.com** for information on our titles

www.ingramcontent.com/pod-product-compliance
Lightning Source LLC
Chambersburg PA
CBHW060524060326
40690CB00017B/3373